VOGUE

SEWING FOR YOUR CHILDREN

VOGUE

SEWING FOR
YOUR CHILDREN

HARPER & ROW, PUBLISHERS, NEW YORK

Cambridge, Philadelphia, San Francisco, Washington
London, Mexico City, São Paulo, Singapore, Sydney

Writer: *Anne Marie Soto*

Illustrator: *Phoebe Adams Gaughan*

Editor: *Helen Moore*

Coordinator for Butterick: *Patricia Perry*

Butterick staff: *Janet DuBane, Carol Sharma, Josephine Gillies, Ron Ferguson, Joanne Cannon*

Coordinator for Harper & Row: *Carol Cohen*

Harper & Row production staff: *Leta Evanthes, Lydia Link, Eric Wirth*

FIRST EDITION

Designed by Jos. Trautwein/Bentwood Studio

Library of Congress Cataloging-in-Publication Data
Vogue sewing for your children.

   Includes index.
   1. Children's clothing.   I. Soto, Anne Marie.
II. Gaughan, Phoebe Adams.   III. Title.
TT635.S69   1987   646.4'06   86-9988
ISBN 0-06-181132-7 (U.S.A. and Canada)
ISBN 0-06-337046-8 (outside U.S.A. and Canada)

87 88 89 90 91 FG 10 9 8 7 6 5 4 3 2 1

Other books from Vogue:

VOGUE SEWING
VOGUE CHRISTMAS
VOGUE DOLLS & TOYS
VOGUE EASY SEWING
VOGUE FITTING
VOGUE SEWING FOR THE HOME

Contents

How to Use This Book

Vogue Sewing for Your Children is designed to give you everything you need to sew for your children—the basics, the latest technological developments and the professional tips that make the basic methods even easier. Wherever possible, the techniques and tools that will save you time and effort have been provided. The emphasis has been placed on sewing children's clothes beautifully, yet easily. The first section, Getting Started, contains the information to help ensure that you'll choose the right size for your child, make the pattern fit properly and find the perfect fabric to sew. The second section, Construction Techniques, includes a complete sewing handbook, arranged in alphabetical order for easy use. You'll also find specific sewing innovations, such as the overlock sewing machine, mentioned throughout the section.

In both sections of the book, you'll see references to various methods or topics at the end of every alphabetical chapter. The terms written in SMALL CAPITAL LETTERS ("For more information see GATHERING") are your signal to refer directly to that topic (in this case Gathering) in the Construction Techniques section. Sometimes, when a Construction Techniques section is long, you are directed to a specific subsection ("For more information on edgestitching, see under MACHINE STITCHING"). In this case, you look up Machine Stitching in the M's, locate the subsection on Edgestitching, and you're all set to sew.

Getting Started

In this busy world of fast-food restaurants, microwave ovens, VCRs, home computers and two-income families, why would anyone want to take the time to sew for children? There are almost as many answers to this question as there are people who sew. Some do it purely for the personal pleasure and relaxation sewing provides. Others do it to create a unique gift of love for someone special. Some sew for economy, scouting fabric sales and remnant tables, creating great treasures at low cost. Still others see it as the best way to perfect a new technique, practicing the art of appliqué, quilting, smocking, etc. on a small scale before using it to enhance their own wardrobe.

No matter why *you* sew for kids, *Vogue Sewing for Your Children* is organized to make your sewing life easier and more pleasurable. It includes:

▶ *how to measure the child accurately to determine the correct size pattern.*

▶ *how to select patterns and fabrics that please both you and the child.*

▶ *how to alter children's patterns, including a special section on the thin and the chubby child.*

▶ *how to incorporate growing room in the garments you sew.*

▶ *construction techniques organized in an A-to-Z format for easy reference.*

▶ *timely information on quick tips, new notions and overlock sewing.*

Are you looking for ways to increase your sewing efficiency, to stretch your clothing dollars or to express your personal sense of creativity? This book can help you do all of these things.

Why Sew for Children?

SAVING TIME

Patterns with fewer pieces mean less time spent cutting, marking and sewing the garment. Read the garment description on the back of the pattern envelope to find out details of the garment which are visible, such as collars and cuffs, as well as those that are invisible, such as side seam pockets or zippers. Study the technical sketches on the back of the envelope or on the catalog page to see the position of seamlines and design lines. In general, simpler styles have fewer pattern pieces. If time is of the essence, and two patterns are similar, pick the one with the fewest pieces.

Using multi-size patterns can eliminate some time-consuming alterations as these patterns are printed with several sizes on one pattern tissue.

Organize your sewing according to the Flat Construction Method. Rather than a garment completed one area at a time, the entire construction sequence is broken down into stages. You complete as many small details as possible on each section of the garment while it is still flat. Then the seams that give the garment its contour, such as side seams, crotch seams and underarm seams, are sewn. This method is particularly well suited to children's wear because once these seams are sewn, the garment can become quite small and some areas may

be difficult to get at on your sewing machine. If your pattern instruction sheet does not follow this method, the section on Flat Construction, page 37, shows you how to adapt your project to this procedure.

Master the techniques for sewing on the overlock machine. These machines stitch, trim and overcast a strong, durable seam, all at the same time—and they do it at a speed that is twice as fast as the fastest conventional sewing machine. Throughout this book, we've included techniques that are applicable to the overlock machine. The section on Overlock Stitching, pages 129–36, provides you with an in-depth look at the various types of overlock machines.

SAVING MONEY

The concept of sewing to save money can mean different things to different people. For some of us, it can mean economizing—shopping carefully for the best price on fabrics, patterns, notions and trims; fashioning leftover fabric from our own wardrobe into children's clothes; or recycling fabric from existing garments that are outdated but not worn out.

For others, it means budgeting the same amount of money we would spend on ready-to-wear clothes, but ending up with better quality, longer lasting,

custom-made garments. And there's an additional bonus—your child will have more clothes for the same amount of money you'd spend on ready-to-wear garments.

EXPRESSING INDIVIDUALITY

Sewing provides you with the opportunity to express your own ideas and creativity. Every time you sew, you become the designer, developing your own unique combination of pattern, color, fabric, notions and trims.

Since the ultimate aim is to create a garment that pleases both you *and* the child, sewing is also an opportunity to express the child's creativity and personality. A child's crayon drawing can be copied in machine embroidery; a hobby or much loved toy can be the inspiration for an appliqué; a favorite color can be featured in the garment.

Involve the child in selecting the pattern, the fabric and/or the color. Children who are encouraged to be involved in the creative process become more interested in how they look and what they wear. As they get older, they may develop an interest in sewing themselves. Many of the most avid sewers we know were inspired by memories of special garments created by mothers, grandmothers and favorite aunts.

Selecting the Right Size and Figure Type

Most children love to run, jump, crawl and climb. They have no tolerance for clothes that are too long or too short, that bind, ride up or are uncomfortable in any way. Although minor fitting adjustments can be taken care of during the sewing process, it's essential to begin by choosing the correct figure type and pattern size.

FIGURE TYPES AND SIZE RANGES

Five of the measurement charts given in the back of the pattern catalog are for children. Once you've taken your child's measurements, you can see which chart has the closest set of measurements and decide on your child's figure type and size.

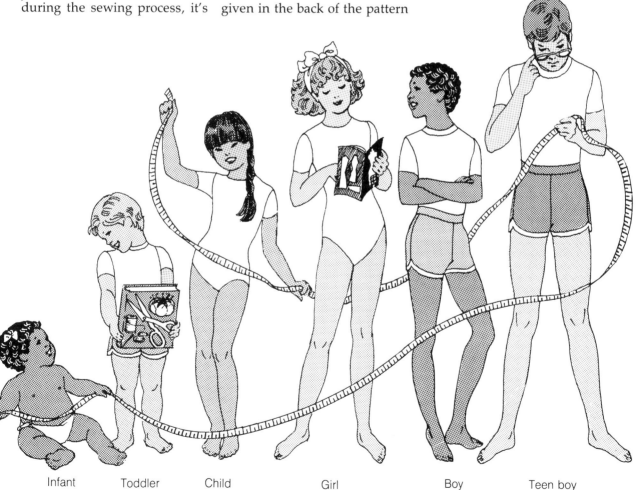

Infant   Toddler   Child   Girl   Boy   Teen boy

13

INFANTS' sizes are meant for babies who are not yet walking. Pattern size is determined by the baby's weight and height.

Size	Newborn	Small	Medium	Large	X-Large
Weight	to 13 lbs. (to 6kg)	13–18 lbs. (6–8kg)	18–22 lbs. (8–10kg)	22–26 lbs. (10–12kg)	26–30 lbs. (12–14kg)
Height	to 24″ (to 60cm)	24–26½″ (60–67cm)	26½–28″ (67–70cm)	28–30½″ (70–76cm)	30½–32″ (76–81cm)

TODDLERS' sizes are designed for the pre-school girl or boy who falls between the Infants' and the Children's sizes. Pattern size is determined by the child's breast or chest and waist measurements. Although the measurements overlap somewhat for Toddlers' and Children's sizes 2, 3 and 4, Toddlers' patterns have extra ease to accommodate bulky diapers and are shorter in length.

Size	Extra Small	Small		Medium	
	½	1	2	3	4
	inches (cm)	inches (cm)	inches (cm)	inches (cm)	inches (cm)
Breast/Chest	19 (48)	20 (51)	21 (53)	22 (56)	23 (58)
Waist	19 (48)	19½ (50)	20 (51)	20½ (52)	21 (53)
Approx. Height	28 (71)	31 (79)	34 (87)	37 (94)	40 (102)

CHILDREN'S sizes are worn by the girl or boy who has outgrown Toddlers' sizes. Height and other length measurements, such as shoulders, arms and garment length, are proportionately longer. Although Toddlers' and Children's sizes 2, 3 and 4 have the same chest and waist measurements, Children are considered slightly taller girls and boys who no longer wear diapers.

Size	Extra Small	Small		Medium		Large
	2	3	4	5	6	6X
	inches (cm)	inches (cm)	inches (cm)	inches (cm)	inches (cm)	inches (cm)
Breast/Chest	21 (53)	22 (56)	23 (58)	24 (61)	25 (64)	25½(65)
Waist	20 (51)	20½ (52)	21 (53)	21½ (55)	22 (56)	22½ (57)
Hip			24 (61)	25 (64)	26 (66)	26½ (67)
Back Waist Length	8½ (22)	9 (23)	9½ (24)	10 (25.5)	10½ (27)	10¾ (27.5)
Approx. Height	35 (89)	38 (97)	41 (104)	44 (112)	47 (119)	48 (122)

GIRLS' sizes are for the child who is too tall for Children's sizes. Although a Girl's figure has not yet begun to mature, she has begun to exhibit a defined waistline.

Size	Small	Medium		Large	
	7	8	10	12	14
	inches (cm)	inches (cm)	inches (cm)	inches (cm)	inches (cm)
Breast	26 (66)	27 (69)	28½ (73)	30 (76)	32 (81)
Waist	23 (58)	23½ (60)	24½ (62)	25½ (65)	26½ (67)
Hip	27 (69)	28 (71)	30 (76)	32 (81)	34 (87)
Back Waist Length	11½ (29.5)	12½ (31)	12¾ (32.5)	13½ (34.5)	14¼ (36)
Approx. Height	50 (127)	52 (132)	56 (142)	58½ (149)	61 (155)

BOYS' and **TEEN BOYS'** sizes fit growing boys and young men who have not yet reached full adult stature.

	BOYS				TEEN BOYS		
	Small	Medium		Large	Small	Medium	Large
Size	7	8	10	12	14	16	18	20
	ins. (cm)	ins. (cm)	ins. (cm)	ins. (cm)	ins. (cm)	ins. (cm)	ins. (cm)	ins. (cm)
Chest	26 (66)	27 (69)	28 (71)	30 (76)	32 (81)	33½ (85)	35 (89)	36½ (93)
Waist	23 (58)	24 (61)	25 (64)	26 (66)	27 (69)	28 (71)	29 (74)	30 (76)
Hip (seat)	27 (69)	28 (71)	29½ (75)	31 (79)	32½ (83)	34 (87)	35½ (90)	37 (94)
Neckband	11¾ (30)	12 (31)	12½ (32)	13 (33)	13½ (34.5)	14 (35.5)	14½ (37)	15 (38)
Approx. Height	48 (122)	50 (127)	54 (137)	58 (147)	61 (155)	64 (163)	66 (168)	68 (173)
Shirt Sleeve	22 (56)	23 (58.5)	25 (63.5)	26 (66)	29 (73.5)	30 (76)	31 (78.5)	32 (81)

MEASURING YOUR CHILD

In order to determine the child's correct pattern size, accurate measurements are a must. To take them, you only need a tape measure, a piece of string or narrow rolled elastic and a child who has been enticed to hold still for a few minutes!

The child should be dressed in underwear (including diapers on a toddler) and standing as naturally as possible. To locate that hard-to-find waistline, tie the string or elastic around the child's waist, then ask the child to bend and stretch a bit. The string will automatically roll into place at the natural waistline.

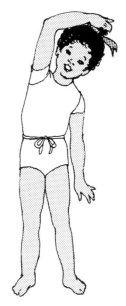

Take the following measurements and record them on the Personal Measurement Chart on page 18. As you take the contour measurements around the body, hold the tape measure snug, but not tight, and parallel to the floor.

1. *Breast/Chest*—*Measure around the fullest part of the chest and straight across the back, just under the shoulder blades (A).*

2. *Waist*—*Measure around the body at the natural waistline, as indicated by the string or elastic (B).*

3. *Hip*—*For* Toddlers' *and* Children's *sizes, measure around their body at the hipbones. For Girls' sizes, measure around their body at the fullest part of their hips (C). For Boys' sizes, measure at their seat or at the fullest part of their hips.*

4. *Back Waist Length*— *Measure from the most prominent bone at the base of the neck to the natural waistline (D). To find the prominent bone, ask the child to bend his or her head forward. You will be able to feel the bone. Place your finger on it and have the child straighten his or her head. Measure from this bone to the natural waistline.*

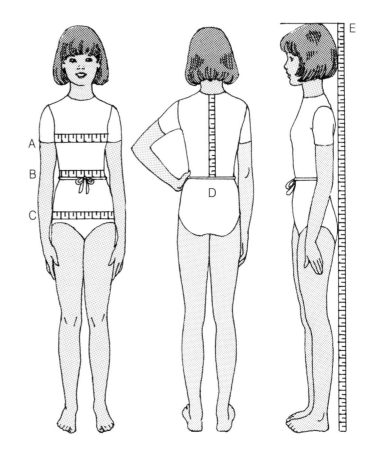

Children grow quickly so be sure to remeasure them before starting each new project.

5. *Height*—*Have the child stand against a wall in stocking feet. Place a ruler on top of the head, parallel to the floor. Then make a mark where the ruler touches the wall. Measure and record height from the floor to the mark (E).*

These additional body measurements will help you refine the fit of the garment. Take them, then measure the pattern tissue and compare. To avoid having to alter the garment later, make any required adjustments on the tissue before the garment is cut out.

6. *Arm Length*—*For* Toddlers, Children *and* Girls, *measure from the top of their arm, over their bent elbow, to their wrist bone (F). For Boys and Teen Boys, measure from the base of the back neck, across the shoulder, around the bend of their elbow, to their wrist bone (G).*

7. *Shoulder Length*—*Measure along the shoulder from the base of the neck to the shoulder bone (H). To find the shoulder bone, have the child raise and lower one arm while you locate the bone with your forefinger.*

16

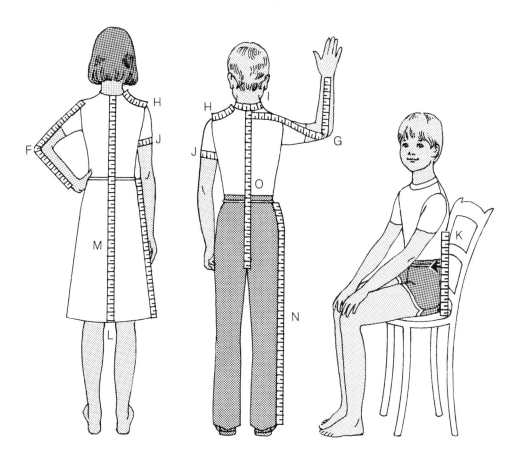

8. Neck—For Boys and Teen Boys only, you'll need to measure the neck to decide on a shirt size. Measure around the base of the neck, at the level of the prominent neck bone (I).

9. Upper Arm—Take this measurement at the fullest part of the upper arm, usually just below the armpit (J).

10. Crotch Depth—Have the child sit on an uncushioned chair, with feet flat on the floor. With a ruler, measure from the string at the side waistline to the seat of the chair (K).

11. Finished Dress Length—Measure from the bone at the base of the back neck to the desired garment length (L).

12. Finished Skirt Length—Measure from the string at the back waistline to the desired garment length (M).

13. Finished Pants Length—Measure from the string at the side waistline to the ankle (N).

14. Finished Jacket Length—Measure from the bone at the base of the back neck to the desired jacket length (O).

If you're faced with a very small—or a very wiggly—child, spare yourself, and the child, by measuring a garment that fits well. It may not be quite as accurate, but it will certainly be easier on you! If you are measuring a pair of pants, rather than the child, you can determine the crotch depth by subtracting the inseam measurement from the outer side seam measurement.

You may not find it necessary to measure or make adjustments in all of the following areas. For young children, you may need to use only the first chart, since their small bodies do not require an exact fit in the areas listed in the second chart. However, for older children whose bodies are more developed, and when working with expensive or fine fabric, you may want to consider taking all of the measurements to achieve a good fit.

Use this chart to record measurements as you take them. Also record the *pattern body measurements* (refer to the charts on pages 14–15) for measurements 1 to 5. Compare the two columns, divide by the appropriate amount and record the amount to adjust.

PERSONAL MEASUREMENT CHART

DATE _____   WEIGHT _____   PATTERN SIZE _____

	Personal Body Measurements	Pattern Body Measurements	Difference (+ or −)	Divide by	Amount to Adjust
1. BREAST/CHEST*					
2. WAIST				4	
3. HIP				4	
4. BACK WAIST LENGTH				0	
5. HEIGHT				0	

	Personal Body Measurements	Pattern Tissue Measurements	Difference (+ or −) / Amount to Adjust	
6. ARM LENGTH				
7. SHOULDER LENGTH				
8. NECK*				
9. UPPER ARM	(+ up to 1⅝″ for ease)			
10. CROTCH DEPTH	(+ up to ⅞″ for ease)			
11. FINISHED DRESS LENGTH				
12. FINISHED SKIRT LENGTH				
13. FINISHED PANTS LENGTH				
14. FINISHED JACKET LENGTH				

Use this chart to compare the child's personal body measurements and the *pattern tissue measurements* for the size and style you've selected. Measure the pattern tissue, seamline to seamline, at the appropriate areas. Record the measurements as well as any differences between the child's body measurements and the pattern tissue. When you are taking body measurements, add extra for ease where indicated on the chart. Add more ease for larger children, less for smaller ones.

Information on pattern adjustments is given on pages 20-25. No adjustments are given for the breast/chest area or the neck area since you select the pattern size closest to those measurements.

Selecting a Pattern

Body measurements, not age, should be your criteria for selecting the pattern size. For a garment with a bodice top (including dresses, shirts, coats and jump suits), purchase the pattern by the breast or chest measurement. For pants, overalls and skirts, purchase the pattern by the waist measurement. For boys and teen boys, purchase shirt patterns by the neck measurement.

The age of the child should influence what styling details you look for in a pattern. Toddlers, whether in or out of diapers, are always scooting, crawling, walking and running. They need clothes that allow them maximum freedom of movement, such as one-piece jumpers and overalls. As children begin to walk more than they crawl, skirts and pants with elasticized waists become a more practical possibility. Pants, skirts and overalls should have shoulder straps that crisscross in the back so that the straps don't fall off the child's shoulders. Shirts with shoulder tabs to hold the straps can serve the same purpose.

Many toddlers take great pride in learning to dress themselves. To encourage this, look for garments with large neck and armhole openings, and large button or snap closings. Oversized pull-tabs can be added to zipper closings. Closures such as hooks and eyes, laces, ties and tiny buttons are best left for special-occasion clothes. Tiny fingers just can't manipulate them.

Preschoolers still need clothes that let them move freely and comfortably, with room to grow. One-piece garments without a waistline, as well as two-piece garments or wrap styles, are the best choices. Look for details such as raglan or kimono sleeves, adjustable shoulder straps and elasticized waist-lines. Large pockets, where kids can stash all sorts of treasures, are particularly appreciated.

Older children may indicate a preference for one style over another. If this is true of your child, involve him or her in selecting the pattern.

Regardless of their ages, it's a good idea to think about making children's clothes that are safe as well as stylish and practical. Avoid anything that might get tangled or cause the child to trip, such as long, flowing skirts or very full sleeves. Tie belts and drawstrings, unless kept very short, are generally not a good idea for babies and toddlers who are beginning to crawl. It's all too easy for the little ones to get tangled up in them.

Small children explore the whole world around them by seeing, feeling and trying to taste the things that capture their attention. Sooner or later, anything that is loose finds its way into their mouths. Buttons, snaps, hooks and eyes, appliqués—anything that decorates or fastens children's clothing—should be sewn on as securely as possible.

When selecting fabrics for children's sleepwear, look for those that are labeled "flame retardant." It's a bit of extra insurance that you'll never regret.

Altering a Pattern

Children's bodies don't have the curves and contours that create fitting problems in adults. If the pattern size is selected to correspond to the child's body measurements, very few pattern alterations, other than lengthening or shortening adjustments, should be necessary. If the child is a different size on the top and the bottom, you can use multi-size patterns to minimize your alterations.

COMPARE ACTUAL BODY TO PATTERN BODY MEASUREMENTS

To find out what, if any, pattern adjustments are required, begin by comparing the child's measurements with the pattern body measurements. Following the guidelines given on pages 15–18, take and record the child's measurements on the chart on page 18.

There's an easy way to determine if any width adjustments are required in the breast/chest, waist or hip area or if the back waist needs to be lengthened or shortened. The basic body measurements for the pattern size you have selected are listed on the back of your pattern envelope. A quick comparison between these measurements and the child's will tell you if, and how much, your child's measurements vary from the pattern body measurements.

To determine if any other changes may be necessary, you'll need to measure the actual pattern tissue, then compare these measurements with the child's body measurements, plus an allowance for ease.

All patterns have a certain amount of ease allowance built into them. **Wearing ease** is the minimum fullness, over and above body measurements, that allows the wearer to move comfortably in the garment. Because many stretch knits have a certain amount of built-in "give," the amount of wearing ease added to a "knits only" garment will be less than the amount of wearing ease added to a garment designed for stable knits or woven fabrics.

To give the garment silhouette the look the designer intended, **design ease** is sometimes added to the garment over and above wearing ease.

IS THIS ADJUSTMENT REALLY NECESSARY?

Before you begin to add or subtract length or fullness to the pattern tissue, study it carefully, analyzing the style of the garment. Use this visual appraisal to help you judge which adjustments may be necessary. For example, the child's waist may differ from what is indicated for the pattern size. If the garment is very full, it may not be necessary to make any adjustments. The child may have a longer or shorter back waist length. A dress without any waistline definition may not require a back waist adjustment. However, for overalls, the back waist length and/or crotch depth would have to be adjusted or the crotch would be uncomfortable.

THE BASICS OF PATTERN ADJUSTMENT

Pattern adjustments are always made on the pattern tissue before the garment is cut out. The process of making accurate pattern adjustments is really quite easy if you follow some simple guidelines:

▶ *Press all pattern pieces with a warm, dry iron to remove the wrinkles and creases before you attempt any adjustments.*

▶ *Mark and pin the adjustment, check it with a tape measure, then pin or tape it carefully in place, using translucent tape you can write on.*

▶ *Make all length adjustments first, then make all width adjustments.*

▶ *Be sure to make all necessary changes on corresponding pattern pieces. For example, if you lengthen the bodice back, you must also lengthen the bodice front; if you add width to the waist and hip area of the front pattern piece, you must also add it to the back.*

▶ *Keep the grainline aligned as you are making each adjustment.*

▶ *Once all the adjustments are completed, double-check each ad-*

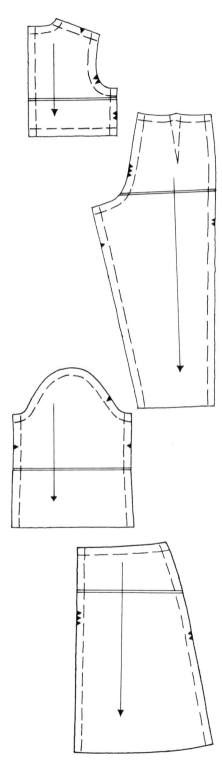

justment and the total circumferences and lengths for accuracy. Note: *The yardage chart on the back of the pattern envelope lists enough yardage to accommodate all of the pattern pieces you'll need, but does not include any extra yardage for longer-length adjustments. Even if you need to make only minor width or length adjustments, you may need to purchase additional fabric.*

MAKING LENGTH ADJUSTMENTS

Using the chart on page 18, compare your child's length measurements (back waist length, arm length, crotch depth, finished garment length) with the pattern tissue. Remember to include ease when comparing crotch depth measurements. Lengthen or shorten the pattern as necessary along the *Lengthen/ Shorten* lines provided on the pattern tissue (as shown).

Once the length adjustments are made, redraw any cutting and construction lines that have been interrupted by the adjustments. If the line is straight, simply place a ruler along the two original lines and connect them. If the line is curved, use a French curve to create a smooth, even line, tapering back to the original lines, or redraw the line freehand.

Be sure to correct any markings on the pattern piece that may have been affected by the adjustment. Buttonholes and other closures may need to be respaced. The position of details such as pockets, casings, trims, darts, bands and appliqués may need to be adjusted.

If the garment has a zipper closing, you may need to purchase a different zipper length.

Lengthening

1. *Locate the appropriate* Lengthen/Shorten *line.*

2. *Cut the pattern tissue apart along this adjustment line.*

3. *Place tissue paper or graph paper underneath.*

4. *Spread the cut pattern edges apart the required amount, keeping the edges parallel.*

5. *Tape or pin the pattern pieces to the paper underneath, making sure that the grainline is still aligned.*

6. *Redraw the interrupted pattern lines and, if necessary, reposition the affected design details (A, B).*

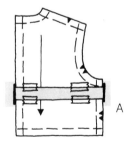

A

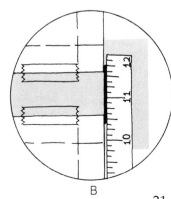

B

21

Shortening

1. *Locate the appropriate* Lengthen/Shorten *line.*

2. *Crease the pattern along the adjustment line and make a fold ½ the amount needed to be shortened.*

3. *Tape or pin the fold in place, making sure that the grainline is still aligned.*

4. *Redraw the interrupted pattern lines and, if necessary, reposition the affected design details (C).*

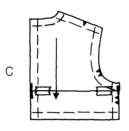

C

MAKING WIDTH ADJUSTMENTS

Width adjustments are usually made by increasing or decreasing the pattern tissue along the side seams. However, if the child is very thin, or very chubby, follow the adjustment procedures on pages 24–25.

To determine the total amount that must be added or subtracted from the pattern, compare the child's measurements with the pattern body measurements, using the chart on page 18. Then determine how much you need to add or subtract along the side seam allowances of the front and the back pattern pieces by dividing the difference by four. Why four? Because the finished garment has two front side seam allowances and two back side seam allowances, for a total of four side seam allowances.

Increasing the Width

1. *Tape or pin a strip of tissue paper to the front pattern piece along the side seam.*

2. *Add ¼ the amount required to the side seam where needed (waistline and/or hipline).*

3. *Redraw the cutting line, tapering it back to meet the original line (as shown on page 23).*

4. *Repeat for the back pattern piece.*

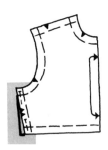

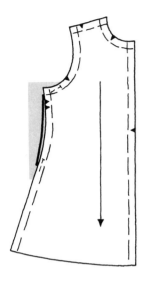

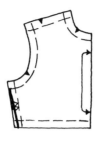

1. *Locate and mark the midpoint of the shoulder seam on the bodice front pattern piece.*

2. *At the mark, slash the tissue from the shoulder cutting line to, but not through, the armhole seamline.*

3. *Tape or pin a strip of tissue paper under one cut edge.*

4. *Spread the cut edges at the shoulder the amount needed, tapering to nothing at the armhole seamline. Tape or pin in place (A). A tuck will form in the armhole seam allowance.*

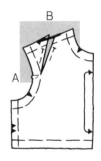

5. *Redraw the cutting lines and seamlines at the shoulder and armhole (B).*

6. *Repeat for the bodice back pattern piece.*

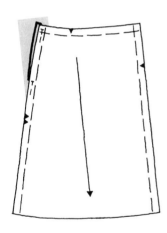

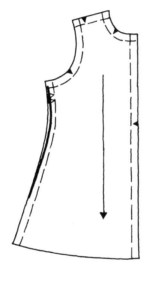

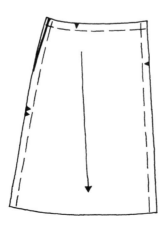

1. *Subtract by making a mark on the front pattern tissue the appropriate distance inside the cutting line, ¼ the amount required.*

2. *Redraw the cutting line, curving it back smoothly to meet the original line (as shown).*

3. *Repeat for the back pattern piece.*

Decreasing Shoulder Width

1. *Locate and mark the midpoint of the shoulder seam on the bodice front pattern piece.*

2. *At the mark, make a fold ½ the amount needed, tapering it to nothing at the armhole seamline. Tape or pin the fold in place (A). You may need to clip the armhole seam allowance slightly to release it.*

3. *Redraw the cutting lines and seamlines at the shoulder and armhole (B).*

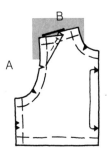

4. *Repeat for the bodice back pattern piece.*

Increasing or Decreasing the Upper Arm Refer to the information that follows on the Thin or Chubby Child for adjustments to increase or decrease the sleeve at the upper arm.

THE THIN OR CHUBBY CHILD

If the child is very thin or very chubby, the width adjustments should be made within the body of the garment, rather than along the side seams.

To determine how much to adjust, compare the child's measurements with the pattern body measurements, using the chart on page 18. The difference between these two measurements will indicate how much the pattern needs to be altered.

On both the chubby and the thin child, the fit in the shoulder area is critical to the overall garment appearance. Be sure to compare the child's shoulder measurement with the pattern tissue measurement. If there is a difference, draw a line from the shoulder to the lower edge on both front and back pattern pieces, and adjust the pattern along the drawn line (A). If no shoulder adjustments are required, draw a line from the armhole to the lower edge and make the width adjustment along the drawn line (B) so that you don't disturb the shoulder line. Be sure, however, to make a corresponding adjustment on the sleeve or armhole facing pattern piece (at the locations indicated by the lines drawn) (C).

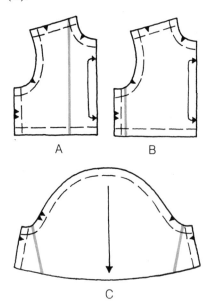

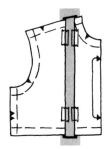

Making the Pattern Smaller for the Thin Child

1. *Analyze the shoulder measurement, as described previously, to determine the appropriate position for the adjustments.*

2. *Crease the pattern along the appropriate line, making a fold that is equal to ⅛ the required decrease.*

3. *Tape or pin the fold and redraw the cutting line, if necessary.*

4. *Repeat this procedure for all corresponding pattern pieces.*

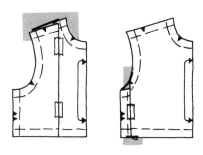

Making the Pattern Larger for the Chubby Child

1. *Analyze the shoulder measurement, as described above, to determine the appropriate position for the adjustments.*

2. *Slash the pattern along the appropriate line.*

3. *Place tissue paper or graph paper underneath.*

4. *Spread the cut pattern edges apart ¼ the required amount, keeping the cut edges parallel. (On the sleeve, the cut edges do not have to be parallel, unless the child has a very heavy arm.)*

5. *Tape or pin the pattern pieces in place.*

6. *Redraw the appropriate cutting lines.*

7. *Repeat this procedure for all corresponding pattern pieces.*

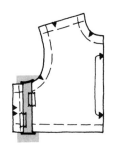

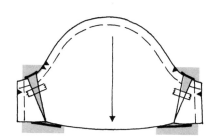

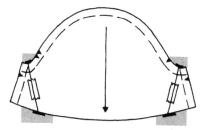

Room to Grow

Children definitely grow like weeds, increasing faster in height than in girth. As a result, garments may become too short long before they get too tight.

Growth allowances can be added to the pattern to accommodate this rapid growth. Before you begin, however, consider carefully whether the quality of the fabric and the life expectancy of the garment warrant this extra effort. In general, it makes the most sense to add growth allowances to dressy clothes (unless they are made from a fabric such as velvet that will show the stitch marks) or sturdy, long-wearing garments such as overalls.

These temporary tucks can be

hidden inside the garment or added to the outside as temporary trim. Don't attempt to add growth tucks to a section of the garment where they will intersect with a button/buttonhole closing. The buttonholes won't be properly spaced once the tucks are released.

Even if you are following the Flat Construction Method, all growth tucks must be constructed after the side seams are sewn.

For easy removal, sew the growth tucks with a long machine basting stitch or with the chain stitch found on some conventional or overlock sewing machines.

OUTSIDE TUCKS

Outside tucks masquerade as decoration, building growing room into just about any children's garment. Even though they are a temporary decoration, tucks should be in proportion to the finished garment and the overall effect should be aesthetically pleasing. If you are adding outside tucks to both the bodice and the skirt, the size and spacing should be the same for all the tucks so that the finished garment has balanced proportions.

Outside growth tucks should be ¼" to ½" (6 to 13mm) deep,

which gives a growth allowance of ½" to 1" (13mm to 2.5cm) per tuck. If they're smaller, they are too narrow to be useful; if they're larger, they begin to look out of proportion to the size of the child.

These tucks are most successful when added to garment sections with rectangular pattern pieces that have straight (on-grain) bottom edges. It is possible to add outside tucks to garments with slightly curved or shaped bottom edges; however, you must take great care to follow the curve *exactly* when drawing the tuck foldlines and stitching lines. Otherwise, the fabric may be pulled off grain and the finished tuck and garment will have a rippled, lumpy look.

Before you adjust the pattern tissue for growth tucks, adjust it to the child's current body measurements, making any necessary pattern adjustments along the *Lengthen/Shorten* line. Then adjust both the front and back pattern pieces for the appropriate growth tucks.

Outside Skirt Tucks

To add the tuck allowance to the pattern tissue:

1. Tape a piece of tissue paper in place along the bottom edge of the pattern piece (A).

2. Mark the finished garment length on the pattern tissue (B).

3. To establish the bottom cutting edge, add together the hem allowance plus twice the depth of each finished tuck. Measure down this amount from the finished garment length and mark the bottom cutting line (C).

4. Extend the side cutting lines and seamlines.

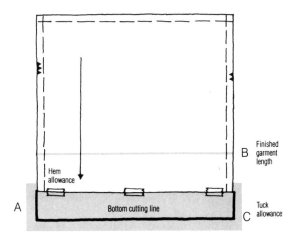

To prepare the garment and mark the tucks:

1. Cut out the skirt from fabric and remove the pattern tissue.

2. On the right side of the fabric, measure up from the bottom edge a distance equal to twice the amount of your hem allowance and mark the hem stitching line (D).

3. Place the first tuck stitching line approximately ½" (13mm) above the hem stitching line and leave about ½" (13mm) between the tucks. Mark the foldline(s) (E) and stitching line(s) (F) for the tuck(s), measuring up from the hem stitching line.

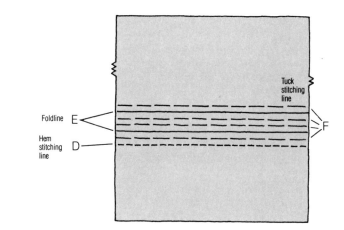

To construct the tucks:

1. Complete the garment, except for the hem.

2. Make the tucks by folding each one along its foldline, matching stitching lines. Stitch the tuck(s).

3. Press each tuck down toward the hemline.

4. As the final step, hem the garment.

Outside Pants Tucks Follow the procedure for Outside Skirt Tucks, above, stitching the tucks after the side seams and inseams are sewn.

Outside Bodice Tucks These tucks can be added to the bodice anywhere between the underarm and the waistline seam. It's up to you to decide where

they will look best for each individual garment. Make sure that the lowest tuck is positioned at least 1" (2.5cm) above the waistline seam.

To add the tuck allowance to the pattern tissue:

1. *Tape a piece of tissue paper in place along the lower edge of the bodice back pattern piece.*

2. *Mark the finished back waist length on the pattern tissue (A).*

3. *To establish the bottom cutting edge, add together the waistline seam allowance plus twice the depth of each finished tuck. Measure down this amount from the finished bodice length and mark the bottom cutting edge (B). Redraw the waistline seam (C).*

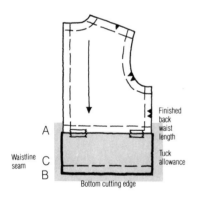

4. *Extend the side cutting lines and seamlines.*

5. *Repeat, making the same adjustments on the bodice front pattern piece.*

To prepare the garment and mark the tucks:

1. *Cut out the bodice from fabric and remove the pattern tissue.*

2. *On the right side of the fabric, measure up from the waistline seam to the first tuck stitching line and mark (D). Then mark the foldline (E) and the second stitching line (F). Continue marking foldlines and stitching lines for the remaining tucks.*

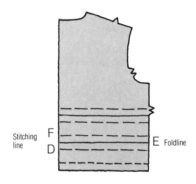

To construct the tucks:

1. *Complete the bodice.*

2. *Make the tucks by folding each one along its foldline, matching stitching lines. Stitch the tuck(s).*

3. *Press each tuck down toward the waistline seam allowance.*

4. *Complete garment, stitching the bodice to the skirt at the waistline seam.*

Outside Sleeve Tucks After you have adjusted your pattern to allow for the extra length, you can position these tucks anywhere you wish on the garment sleeve, from slightly below the underarm seam to 1" (2.5cm) above the sleeve hem stitching line.

Follow the same procedure as for Outside Skirt Tucks, above, stitching the tucks after the sleeve underarm seam is sewn.

INSIDE TUCKS

An inside tuck is one deep growth tuck that is concealed on the wrong side of the garment. On a skirt, the inside tuck is incorporated into the hem allowance. That means you don't have to restitch the hem after you release the tuck. An inside hem tuck can be ½" to 2" (13mm to 5cm) deep. However, it should always be narrower than the width of the hem allowance so that it doesn't peek out beneath the hemline.

Within the bodice area, position an inside tuck just above the waistline seam or, on a one-piece garment, just above the natural waistline. These tucks can be ¼" to ¾" (6mm to 20mm) deep.

Inside tucks are most successful on garment sections with rectangular pattern pieces and straight (on-grain) lower edges.

Adding an inside tuck to a very curved or shaped hem allowance may have unsatisfactory results. The extra layers of fabric may require a great deal of easing to lie flat, resulting in a ripply, messy-looking tuck and hem.

Before you adjust the pattern tissue for inside growth tucks, adjust the pattern to the child's current body measurements, making any necessary pattern adjustments along the *Lengthen/Shorten* line. Adjust both the front and back pattern pieces for the appropriate growth tucks.

Inside Skirt Tucks

To add the tuck allowance to the pattern tissue:

1. *Add a piece of tissue paper to the bottom of the skirt pattern piece and tape in place (A).*

2. *Mark the finished garment length on the tissue (B).*

3. *To establish the bottom cutting edge, add together the hem allowance plus twice the depth of the finished tuck. Measure* down *this amount from the finished garment length and mark the bottom cutting line (C).*

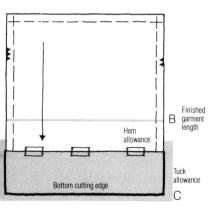

4. *Extend the side cutting lines and seamlines.*

To prepare the garment and mark the tuck:

1. *Cut out the skirt from fabric and remove the pattern tissue.*

2. *On the right side of the fabric, mark the finished garment length (D) and measure* up *from the cutting edge to mark the first tuck stitching line (E), the tuck foldline (F) and the second tuck stitching line (G). Make sure that the first tuck stitching line (E) is at least ½" (13mm) away from the raw edge so that the tuck can be released without removing the hem.*

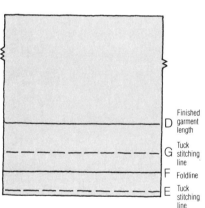

D Finished garment length
G Tuck stitching line
F Foldline
E Tuck stitching line

To construct the tuck:

1. *Complete the garment, except for the hem.*

2. *Fold fabric to the inside along the marking for the finished garment length and press.*

3. *Make the tuck by folding along the foldline, matching stitching lines. Stitch the tuck.*

4. *Press the tuck down toward the hemline.*

5. *Hem the garment.*

Inside Pants Tucks Follow the same procedure as for Inside Skirt Tucks, above, stitching the tucks after the side seams and inseams are sewn, but before hemming the pants.

On a one-piece garment, you might want to add a piece of trim to the right side of the garment to hide the seamline of the inside growth tuck. Be sure to remove the trim before you release the tuck.

Inside Bodice Tuck This type of tuck provides growing room in the waist-to-armhole area on garments with or without a waistline seam. It is positioned slightly above the waistline seam so that it can be easily removed once the child grows. Before beginning, review the general information for Inside Tucks.

To add the tuck allowance to the pattern tissue:

1. *On a one-piece garment, first mark the waistline by drawing a line across the pattern tissue at the waistline marking.*

2. *Next, draw a line across the pattern piece that is 1" (2.5cm) above the waistline seam, or waistline marking, and perpendicular to the center front or center back. Cut the pattern tissue apart along this line.*

3. *Place tissue paper or graph paper underneath.*

4. *Spread the cut pattern edges apart a distance equal to twice the depth of the finished tuck (A), keeping the cut edges parallel.*

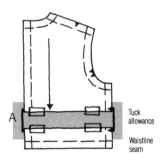

A — Tuck allowance

Waistline seam

5. *Tape the pattern pieces in place, making sure the grainline and/or center foldline is still aligned.*

6. *Redraw the side cutting lines and seamlines.*

To prepare the garment and mark the tuck:

1. *Cut out the garment from fabric.*

2. *Working on the wrong side of the fabric, measure up about 1/16" to 1/8" (2mm to 3mm) from the waistline marking, or waistline seam, and mark the first tuck stitching line (B). Then measure up twice the depth of the finished tuck and mark the second tuck stitching line (C). Mark the foldline halfway between the tuck stitching lines (D).*

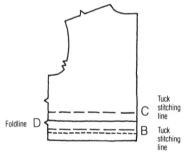

Foldline D

C — Tuck stitching line

B — Tuck stitching line

To construct the tuck:

1. *Assemble the bodice.*

2. *Make the tuck by folding along the foldline, matching stitching lines. Stitch the tuck.*

3. *Press the tuck up, toward the bodice.*

4. *Finish constructing the garment. As you attach the bodice to the skirt, be careful not to catch the tuck in your stitching.*

SHOULDER TUCKS

Shoulder tucks can be either outside or inside tucks. Whichever style you choose, you'll be happiest with the finished look if you add two 1/8" (3mm)-wide tucks to *each* shoulder so the finished garment is visually balanced. And, you'll be able to enlarge the shoulder area in two stages. First, the garment can be widened 1/2" (13mm) by releas-

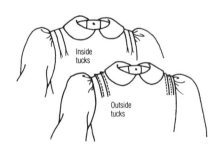

Inside tucks

Outside tucks

ing one tuck at each shoulder. Later on, the garment can be widened another ½" (13mm) by releasing the remaining two tucks.

Outside Shoulder Tucks The additional fullness created by the tucks becomes part of the overall garment design. Be sure to make adjustments on both the bodice front and the bodice back.

To add the tuck allowance to the pattern tissue:

1. *Locate and mark the midpoint of the shoulder seam on the bodice front pattern piece.*

2. *From this midpoint, using a T square or an L square, draw a line 3" (7.5cm) long, perpendicular to the shoulder seam (A). Now draw a second line that extends from the tip of the first line to the armhole. This second line should be parallel to the shoulder seam (B).*

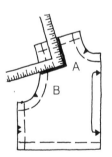

3. *Beginning at the midpoint of the shoulder seam, cut the pattern tissue apart along these two lines, cutting to, but not through, the armhole stitching line (C).*

4. *Insert a piece of tissue paper underneath the cut lines of the*
pattern. Spread the pattern so that the cut edges are ½" (13mm) apart at the shoulder seam and tape in place.

5. *Redraw the cutting lines and seamlines at the shoulder (D).*

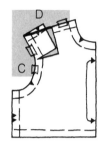

6. *Repeat for the bodice back pattern piece.*

To prepare the garment and mark the tucks:

1. *Cut out the bodice from fabric and remove the pattern tissue.*

2. *On the right side of the fabric, locate the midpoint of the shoulder seam (E). Make two marks ¼" (6mm) to each side of the midpoint. At each of these marks, draw a line 3" (7.5cm) long, perpendicular to the shoulder seam for your tuck foldlines (F).*

3. *Now draw lines on either side of each tuck foldline that are ⅛" (3mm) from, and parallel to, the foldline. These are your tuck stitching lines (G).*

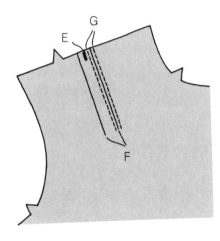

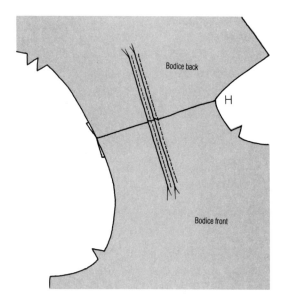

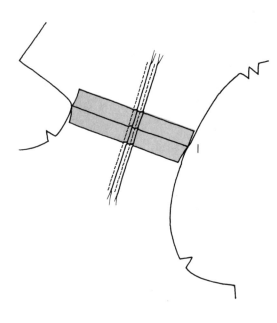

To construct the tucks:

1. *Stitch the shoulder seams of the bodice, and press open.*

2. *Working on the outside of the bodice, make the tucks by folding each tuck along its foldline, matching stitching lines. Stitch the tucks.*

3. *Press each tuck toward the armhole seam (H).*

4. *Complete the garment.*

Inside Shoulder Tucks With these tucks, the growth allowance is hidden on the inside of the garment. Be sure to make all adjustments on both the front and back bodice sections.

Follow the same procedure as for Outside Shoulder Tucks, pages 31–32, making all markings and stitching on the inside of the garment (I).

REMOVING TUCKS

To release growth tucks that intersect with a zipper closing, remove the stitching at the lower end of the zipper, then remove the stitches that form the tuck(s). Stitch the seam closed beneath the bottom stop of the zipper, then restitch the lower end of the zipper in place.

Once the tucks are removed, make sure that no traces of the original foldlines or stitching lines remain.

Using your seam ripper, carefully remove the stitches, then press out any creases. Press carefully on the right *and* wrong side of the garment, using the maximum amounts of steam and heat that are appropriate for your fabric. If stitch impressions remain, especially on napped fabrics, try brushing them out with a small clothes brush or an old toothbrush. If crease marks remain, try using a white vinegar and water solution as described on page 42.

If none of this works, it's time to indulge in a little fashion camouflage. Cover up those telltale lines with lace, rickrack, braid, rows of machine embroidery or appliqués.

Once you have covered up the lines, step back and take a good look at the garment. Does the new trim look like part of the overall design or does it look like a patch-up job? If the latter is true, you probably need to provide balance by repeating the new trim in another part of the garment. It might mean a touch of embroidery added to the collar, some rickrack added to the sleeves or a bit of lace added at the neckline.

THE EXPANDABLE WAISTLINE

An elastic casing can be added to the back waistline on any dress, pants or jumpsuit with a waistline seam. In the first stages of growth, the elastic will stretch to provide additional room. Once the elastic gets too tight, it can be removed, making the garment 2″ (5cm) larger at the waist.

To adjust the pattern tissue:

1. *Tape a piece of tissue paper in place along the side edge of the bodice back pattern piece.*

2. *Add 1" (2.5cm) to the side seam at the waistline (A).*

3. *Redraw the cutting line and seamlines, tapering back to the underarm (B).*

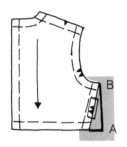

4. *Repeat for the skirt or pants back pattern piece, tapering to the original cutting lines and seamlines at the lower edge of the garment (C). (Note: If garment has a gathered skirt, it is not necessary to alter the skirt back pattern piece, since you can adjust the gathers to fit.)*

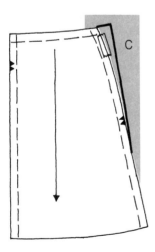

To construct the garment:

1. *Cut out the garment sections from fabric.*

2. *Sew the center back seam (if any). Then, sew the bodice back to the skirt or pants back.*

3. *Cut a piece of extra-wide single-fold bias tape that is ¾" (20mm) smaller than the back waistline pattern measurement. (Be sure to measure the pattern tissue along the waistline seam between the stitching lines, not the cutting lines.) Press the tape under ⅝" (15mm) at each short end.*

4. *Fold the right side of the bodice toward the right side of the skirt or pants.*

5. *Open out one long fold of bias tape. Place the right side of the tape on the waistline seam allowance so that the short ends are 1" (2.5cm) in from the side seamlines and the crease is just above the waistline seam. Sew in place at the crease, stitching through the seam allowance area only (A).*

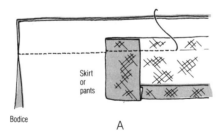

6. *To reduce bulk, trim the waistline seam allowance to ¼" (6mm) and machine zigzag, overcast or overlock stitch.*

7. *Press the bodice away from the skirt or pants. Press the tape up toward the bodice and pin it in place. Edgestitch the tape along the upper edge, stitching through the tape and the bodice back (B).*

8. *Cut a piece of ½" (13mm)-wide elastic that is ¾" (20mm) shorter than the child's back waist measurement. Insert the elastic into the casing, with the ends extending past the casing, and stitch across both short ends of the casing, catching and securing the elastic (C).*

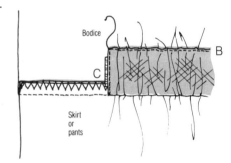

To expand the garment, simply remove the stitches at the ends of the bias casing and pull out the elastic.

OTHER GROWTH OPTIONS

Extra-wide Seam Allowances

Side seam allowances can be expanded from ⅝" (15mm) to 1" (2.5cm) on garments without a waistline seam or waistband. You can enlarge the garment up to 1½" (3.8cm) by letting out the side seams ⅜" (10mm). Be sure to add the extra amount to the sleeve or facing underarm

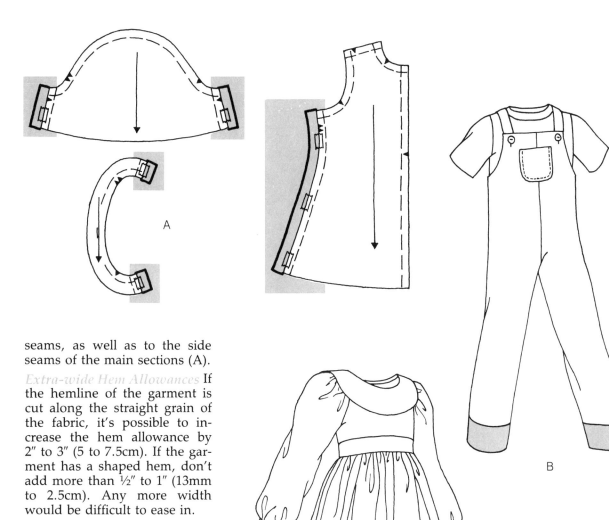

seams, as well as to the side seams of the main sections (A).

Extra-wide Hem Allowances If the hemline of the garment is cut along the straight grain of the fabric, it's possible to increase the hem allowance by 2″ to 3″ (5 to 7.5cm). If the garment has a shaped hem, don't add more than ½″ to 1″ (13mm to 2.5cm). Any more width would be difficult to ease in.

Adding Trim to the Lower Edge Consider adding a band (B) or ruffle of matching or contrasting fabric (C) to the lower edges of skirts, dresses, pants and sleeves. Pregathered eyelet added to the bottom of a skirt can give the illusion of a pretty petticoat peeking out underneath.

Straps That Grow On garments with shoulder straps, cut the straps a little longer, then adjust the length by repositioning the buttons as needed.

Fabric Selection

Children's clothing should be made from fabrics that are long-lasting, comfortable and easy to care for. The most durable fabrics are those that are firmly woven, such as denim and broadcloth, and those that are firmly knitted, such as single and double knits. Other good choices include gingham, chambray, poplin, percale, synthetic linen, sailcloth, piqué, seersucker, madras and corduroy. Tweeds, lightweight wools and fake furs make warm, durable jackets and coats.

If the fabric in a child's garment cannot survive frequent washings, the garment may be "washed out" long before it's worn out. Many children also go through a stage where they develop an attachment to one particular item of clothing, wearing it again and again. Everyone is happier if it can be quickly cleaned and returned to the child. For easy care, choose fabrics marked "permanent press," "soil retardant," "stain repellent," "colorfast" and "shrink resistant."

Safety is another important factor. Dark colors may not be a good idea for outerwear garments like raincoats and jackets because they make the child hard to see at night. However, if you do use a dark color, consider adding strips or patches of reflective or fluorescent tape to make the child more visible. When choosing fabrics for sleepwear, it's wise to look for those that are inherently flame-retardant, such as wool or modacrylic, or those that have a flame-retardant finish.

Most children are particularly fond of bright, primary colors, especially red. In fact, red and yellow are the first two colors a baby can recognize. Kids also like prints, plaids and stripes. It's generally best to stick to the smaller-scale ones that are in proportion to the child's size.

Children are also attracted to fabrics that are soft to touch, such as flannel, corduroy, terry cloth, velvet and velveteen (the washable versions, of course!). Avoid scratchy trims and fabrics such as rough wools or metal-lics, or those with slubbed surfaces, that will irritate a child's sensitive skin.

Many fabrics that require special handling, such as quilted or napped textures, fake furs or vinyls and synthetic leathers, should also be considered. They're fun for the child to wear and a skill-building sewing experience for you. For special handling procedures, refer to Fabrics, pages 90–95.

What to Know Before You Sew

Preplanning is the key to simplified sewing. Even before you lay out the pattern, spend a few minutes reviewing the instruction sheet. Decide which marking technique is best for your fabric and pattern. Collect the marking and pressing equipment you will need. To make sewing easier, consider using the Flat Construction Method, pages 99–100. If you need to review any sewing techniques—or there are some that are new to you—refer to Construction Techniques.

GETTING ORGANIZED

If you follow the step-by-step procedures exactly as they are written on your pattern instruction sheet, you can't go wrong. However, as your sewing expertise develops, you will be able to speed up your sewing by reorganizing some sewing procedures, using the Assembly Line or Flat Construction Methods.

The Assembly Line Method
Save time and energy by rearranging the steps for constructing a garment so that you do all similar activities at the same time. For example:

▶ *Cut out and mark everything—fashion fabric, lining, interfacing, etc.—at one time.*

▶ *Fuse or baste all the interfacings in place at one time.*

▶ *Prefinish the seam allowances before you sew the seams together. Use the continuous stitching method that follows as you finish the seams.*

▶ *Stitch as many seams as you can, in all different parts of the garment, in one sitting. Then head for the ironing board to press them.*

▶ *Use continuous stitching wherever you can, going immediately from one seam to another without stopping in between to cut or tie off threads. If you want to secure the ends of each seam, backstitch a few stitches, then continue sewing.*

▶ *If you own an overlock machine, maximize its use. Keep in mind that the overlock seam should be used on garments you won't alter later.*

The Flat Construction Method
This method can be used hand in hand with the Assembly Line Method. Simply complete as much detail work as possible, such as constructing and attaching pockets, placket bands and collars or applying trims and appliqués, on each garment section before joining sections together along major seamlines. It is easier to do these things when the garment sections are flat before the side seams are sewn. You sew the side seams, from sleeve edge to hem edge, when the garment is almost completed. (See the Flat Construction Method, pages 99–100.)

MARKING

Accurate marking is an absolute necessity. Marking symbols, such as large solid circles ●,

To further increase your sewing efficiency, cut out and mark all fabrics and fuse or baste interfacings in place *on more than one child's* sewing project at a time.

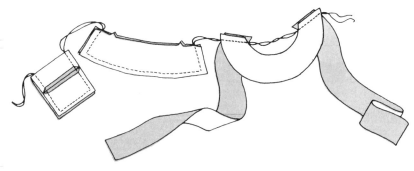

Clip marking, making small scissor snips within the seam allowance to mark the notch location, is not recommended for children's wear. As the child grows, you may want to let out some of the seams. If you have clip marked, you won't be able to do it!

small solid circles ●, squares ■ and triangles ▲, vary from pattern company to pattern company. However, your instruction sheet will identify them for you. These symbols, along with darts (A), placement lines (B), foldlines (C), tuck or pleat lines (D) and button and buttonhole indications (E), should be marked. The notches along the cutting lines are another kind of symbol which you should have already "marked" by cutting around them as you cut out the pattern.

Transfer the markings to the fabric after the garment pieces are cut out, but before the pattern tissue is removed. Choose the quickest, easiest method that is suitable for your fabric from these techniques.

For super-quick marking, there are pens which make markings that disappear. The ink evaporates from the fabric, usually in less than 48 hours. When using these pens, mark just before you sew.

Tracing Paper and Tracing Wheel For the most satisfactory results, use this marking method on firmly woven or knitted, opaque fabrics.

Tracing paper is available in an assortment of colors. Insert the tracing paper between the layers of fabric and pattern tissue, with the coated side of the paper against the wrong side of your fabric. Many tracing papers leave marks that are not removable, but some of the newer ones make marks that are water soluble. These water soluble papers can be used to transfer the markings to either the right or the wrong side of washable fabric. To mark two layers of fabric at one time, fold paper in half with the coated side in and place around the fabric layers.

It's not necessary to mark all the stitching lines on your fabric, although you should mark them in tricky areas or in places where the fabric will cover the stitching guidelines on your machine's throat plate.

If your sewing machine throat plate isn't marked for various seam widths, make your own seam guide by placing a piece of tape to the right of the needle. Measure from the needle and mark it for ½" (13mm), ⅝" (15mm), ¾" (20mm) and 1" (2.5cm) seam widths.

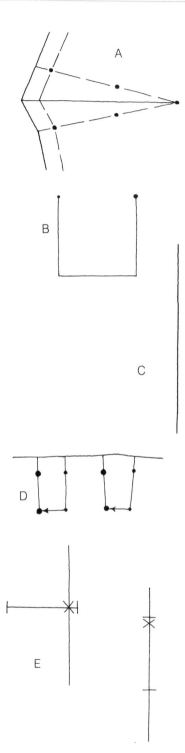

Press firmly on the tracing wheel as you transfer the markings. A piece of cardboard slipped under your fabric protects your work surface and makes your markings clearer. When tracing straight lines, use a straight-edged ruler as a guide. Mark an X on dots, squares or dart points. Do not use this method on sheers because the markings will show through.

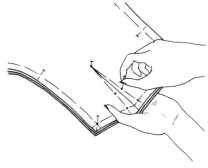

Pretest the tracing paper on a scrap of your fabric:

■ Make sure your choice of colored tracing paper is as close to the fabric color as possible but still clearly visible on your fabric.

■ If your tracing paper makes water soluble markings, test the removal procedure to make sure the markings disappear completely.

To clean your iron, use one of the commercial iron-cleaning solutions and an old cotton sock or worn-out washcloth.

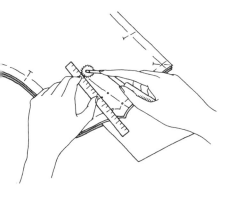

Water Soluble Marking Pens These pens make marks that are removable with plain water. For best results, test them first and use them only on washable fabrics. Using pins, follow the same method as for *tailor's chalk* to locate the position of the markings. Mark on the right or the wrong side of the fabric.

Pins and Tailor's Chalk Test first to make sure the chalk marks are visible on your fabric. If you wish to transfer some of the markings, such as tuck lines or pocket placements, to the right side of the fabric, make sure the chalk brushes off without a trace. Also test whether or not the pins leave holes or cause runs in the fabric.

To mark, first push pins straight down at all marking points through both the pattern tissue and the layers of fabric. Hold the pins and fabric together firmly while gently pulling the tissue over and away from the pin head, making a *small* hole in the tissue. Make a chalk mark at each pin on the wrong side of each fabric layer.

A PRESSING ISSUE

No amount of dexterity at your sewing machine hides the fact that you didn't follow the press-as-you-sew rule. The good news is that careful pressing makes a novice home sewer look like a pro.

Every seam, dart, etc. should be pressed in a two-step operation:

First, press the seam or dart flat on one side, then turn the fabric over and press again on the other side. This blends the stitches.

Then, press the seam allowances open, up, down or to one side, as the pattern instructions specify.

Press darts and seams before other stitching crosses them.

This prevents unwanted thickness and an untidy appearance on the outside of the garment.

Press on the wrong side of the fabric whenever you can. If you must press on the right side, use a press cloth to prevent marks and shiny spots.

Pressing Equipment The essentials are a good, adjustable-heat steam iron, preferably one with a burst-of-steam button, and an adjustable-height ironing board. In addition, there are pressing aids that will help you achieve professional results.

standard ironing board when sewing for children.

A **tailor's ham** is called just that because it's shaped somewhat like the ham you buy from your butcher. The firmly stuffed cushion has rounded surfaces for pressing the shaped and curved areas of a garment, such as darts and sleeve caps. One side is covered with wool so that it absorbs and holds steam. The other side is covered with a tightly woven cotton which makes it useful for pressing all fabrics, whether or not steam is required.

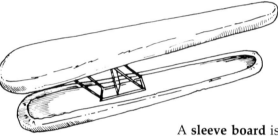

A **sleeve board** is a miniaturized, usually collapsible, version of the standard ironing board, with two pressing surfaces. Small seams and details can be pressed easily on a sleeve board. You may find that the sleeve board is more useful for general pressing than your

A **press mitt** is the sewer's variation of the potholder. Because it has pockets, you can slip it over your hand or over the end of the sleeve board. Like the tailor's ham, it is used to press shaped or curved surfaces. However, its small size makes it

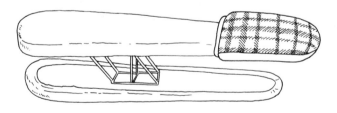

If you keep your sleeve board and your iron on a low table within arm's reach of your sewing machine, you can do some of your pressing without ever getting up from the machine.

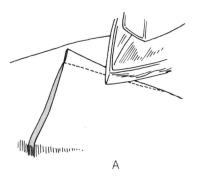

A

especially useful for pressing children's clothes.

A **seam roll** is used to press small, hard-to-reach curves and long seams. It looks like a large, tightly packed sausage. Like the tailor's ham, one side is covered with wool, the other side with a tightly woven cotton. It is particularly useful for pressing children's garments because some curved areas are too small to fit over the ham.

A **press cloth** protects your fabric from scorch marks and iron shine. Commercial press cloths are available in several weights—use the one that is similar in weight to your fashion fabric. Press cloths can be used dry or they can be dampened when you need to create additional steam.

A **point presser** is a wooden pressing tool made up of many differently shaped surfaces. Almost any size point, curve or

straight edge can be pressed by fitting it over one of these surfaces. Because these surfaces are all fairly narrow, these areas can be pressed flat and open without wrinkling the surrounding area.

Pressing Darts Because darts give fit and shape to a garment, they should be pressed on one of the curved pressing aids, such as a tailor's ham, seam roll or press mitt, to maintain the curved shape.

Begin by pressing the dart flat, first on one side, then on the other. To prevent adding any unwanted creases to the garment, press just to the point of the dart (A). Then press the dart to one side or slash and press open, as indicated on your pattern instruction sheet. If the dart is slashed, press it open using a press cloth and the tip of your iron. Start at the widest part of the dart and work toward the point (B). As a general rule, press vertical darts toward the center front or center back and horizontal darts downward. Press the darts before they are crossed by a seam.

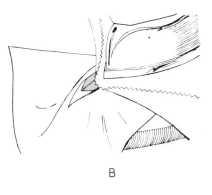

B

Scraps of your garment fabric can substitute for a purchased press cloth. Layers of cheesecloth also make good seethrough press cloths. A man's handkerchief also makes a nice small press cloth, especially if you need to dampen it for extra steam.

Brown wrapping paper or paper bags can be cut into strips and placed under seam; dart and hem edges when you press from the wrong side to prevent edges from making imprints on the right side.

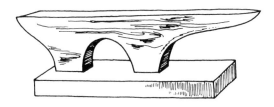

Are you stuck with a crease that won't press out? Try spraying it with a solution of equal parts of white vinegar and water. Then press over a press cloth. If that doesn't work, try white vinegar alone. Pretest this technique on a scrap of the fabric to be sure it can tolerate vinegar. Then rinse to remove the vinegar.

Pressing Gathers Gathers should be pressed carefully to avoid adding creases or wrinkles to the area. Begin by using the tip of your iron to press the gathers flat within the seam allowance area only (A). Then, still using only the tip of your iron, press the seam allowances in the direction indicated on your instruction sheet. Seam allowances are generally pressed away from the gathers for a flat look and toward the gathers for a puffier look.

To finish pressing, hold the garment section along the line of gathering stitches and press from below the gathers toward the stitching. As you near the gathers, use the tip of the iron to press between the fabric folds (B).

Pressing Hems The hem allowance should be steamed and pressed into place before the hem is hand or machine stitched.

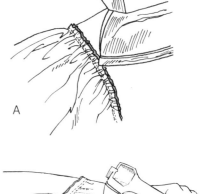

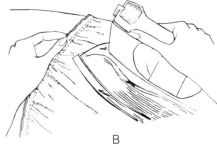

A

B

If the hem is curved or shaped, steaming helps you ease the excess fabric fullness in the hem allowance.

To prevent marks, place strips of brown paper between the hem and the garment. Hold the iron about 3" (7.5cm) above the fabric, then steam and press lightly (C). Do not press over pins or basting thread. After the hem is sewn, steam it lightly (D). If you want a crisp hem edge, press it firmly, using a press cloth.

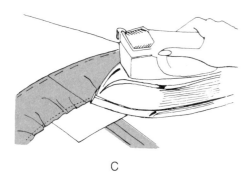

C

Make your own seam roll by covering a tightly rolled magazine with fabric or by wrapping a rolling pin with a towel.

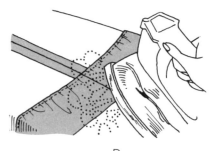

D

Pressing Pleats The type of pleat and the look—crisp or soft—determine which pressing method to use.

Crisp Pleats: For crisp pleats after basting, press them lightly on both the right and wrong sides, just enough to set the pleats without permanently creasing them. As you press, place strips of brown paper under the pleat folds. Use a press cloth and a small amount of steam. Let the garment cool and have the child try it on to make sure the pleats hang correctly.

To set the pleats permanently, use steam, the paper strips and a press cloth to press the pleats to within 5″ (12.5cm) of the lower edge (E). Later on, after the garment is hemmed, go back and press the rest of the creases into the lower edges of the pleats.

Soft Pleats: Set these pleats with steam from your iron rather than by pressing. Pin the pleats in place on your ironing board cover. Holding the iron 2″ to 3″ (5 to 7.5cm) from the pleats, steam them. Allow the fabric to cool and thoroughly dry before removing it from the ironing board (F).

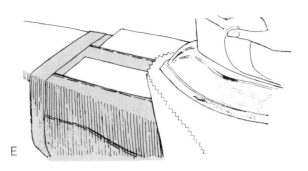

E

Hemline Pleats: If these pleats fold on a seam line, they often fall open or don't hang in place properly. You can correct this by careful pressing before hemming the garment.

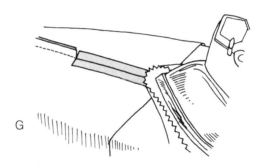

G

Clip the pleat seam at the top of the hem allowance and press open the seam allowance below

the clip (G). Trim the seam allowance within the hem area. Turn the hem up and fold the pleat underfold along the seam. Press a sharp crease in the underfold, using steam and a press cloth. If the fold still falls open, secure it by stitching close to the edge and press again (H).

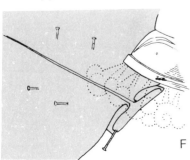

F

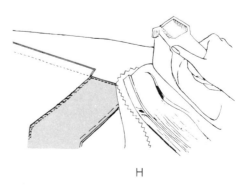

H

Pressing Seams Use the contours of your seam as a guide to deciding which pressing aid to use.

Flat Seams: Use a seam roll when pressing these seams or place strips of brown paper between the seam allowance and the garment. Open the seam with the tip of your iron. If your fabric reacts well to it, use steam as you press and protect your fabric with a press cloth (A).

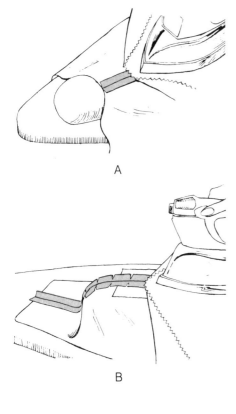

A

B

Curved Seams: Like most other seams, these should be pressed open. However, you want to press in such a way that the natural contours aren't removed. Clip the seam allowance at intervals to help flatten it. Use either a tailor's ham or a press mitt as your pressing surface—it will help you maintain that shape. Put brown paper strips under the seam allowances and use a press cloth between the seam and your iron (B).

Enclosed Seams: When seam allowances are enclosed in the finished garment, they should be pressed flat, then open, before they are turned and pressed. This procedure makes turning the garment section to the right side much easier and helps give a defined edge that won't shift or roll.

Enclosed seams are found on facings, cuffs, collars, pocket flaps, belts and sashes. Because the seam areas are often small, use one of the edges of a point presser for easy access. Using the tip of the iron, open up seam allowances and press (C).

C

Place the garment section flat with the underside up. Gently fold the seam allowances to the side you are pressing until you can just see the stitching line and press lightly in place (D).

Now turn the garment section right side out and press. To protect the fabric, use a press cloth during this final pressing (E).

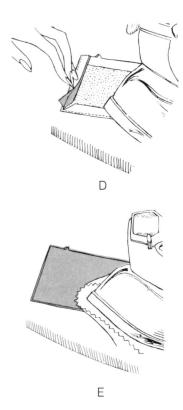

D

E

Pressing Sleeves If you are not using the Flat Construction Method, pages 99–100, follow these pressing techniques.

Use a sleeve board or seam roll when pressing the sleeve seam open (A).

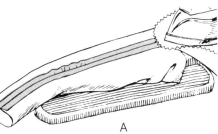

A

Once you have eased and fitted the sleeve cap into the armhole by adjusting the fullness along the gathering threads, remove the sleeve from your garment. To maintain its shape, work on the right side of the sleeve cap, pressing it over the curved surface of a press mitt. With steam, shrink the extra fullness from the seam allowance only by using just the tip and edges of your iron (B).

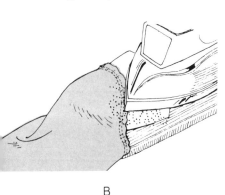

B

After you have stitched the sleeve into the garment, press the seam allowance on the finished sleeve. Place it over a tailor's ham and press along the seam, using very little steam (C). Avoid the sleeve cap area so you don't press in unnecessary creases.

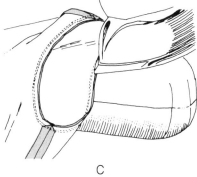

C

Final Pressing Your completed garment should get one last pressing—a light one to smooth and remove any surface wrinkles that may have formed during finishing. Some areas may require a little steam to set them and give them shape. Maintain the shape by padding these areas with tissue paper and letting the garment hang until the fabric dries.

For hard-to-reach enclosed seams in narrow areas, such as tubing, drawstrings and narrow sashes, insert a thin wooden dowel—or a chopstick—before pressing the seam open. Turn tubing, etc., right side out and insert dowel again for final pressing.

Use a metal hem guide to evenly trim and press your hem allowance at one time. Working on the wrong side of your garment, position the hem guide so that one edge is along the hemline of the garment. Fold the hem allowance up over the guide and press. Then, using the markings on the guide, trim the hem allowance to the desired width. *Caution: Keep a potholder handy. Because the hem guide is metal, it may get hot.*

Construction
Techniques

Appliqué

Appliqué is the art of embellishing a large piece of fabric with a smaller, shaped piece of fabric to create a raised effect. You can add a distinctive personal touch by choosing designs for appliqués that reflect the child's hobbies, much loved toy or favorite storybook or cartoon character.

Resources for appliqué designs are plentiful: children's storybooks or coloring books, cookie cutters and greeting cards are all sources of ideas and patterns.

Commercial appliqués are available in a variety of motifs, from flowers and initials to sports themes and small figures or animals. Some of them have a fusible backing for quick, easy application.

Appliqué patches can be used to cover up a worn spot or to provide extra reinforcement in areas that are subject to a great deal of wear and abrasion, such as elbows and knees.

As a general rule, if the appliqué is functioning as a patch, the appliqué fabric should be durable and the design simple. Commercially made, iron-on

---

For knee patches that are comfortable as well as functional, use quilted fabrics, or pad the appliqué with a layer of quilt batting or polyester fleece.

---

mending patches are also available in a variety of sizes and functional shapes. For a more fanciful look, cut these patches into simple decorative shapes. Apply these patches with an iron, according to the manufacturer's directions. Although machine zigzag stitching is not necessary, you may wish to add it as a more secure finishing touch.

MACHINE APPLICATION

The sturdiest way to attach an appliqué to a garment is by machine. Cut out the appliqué pieces to their exact finished size. Seam allowances are not required. Baste the appliqué in position. Then use a smooth, even machine zigzag stitch to permanently attach the appliqué as explained in the instructions that follow.

Basting the Appliqué To prevent the appliqué from shifting and rippling as you sew, baste it securely in place with fusible web or glue stick.

If the appliqué design contains shapes that overlap, think of the design as a series of layers. Begin by basting the bottom layer first, and build up to the top layer. In most cases, the larger parts of the appliqué are applied first and the smaller, more detailed sections last.

Fusible Web: Test fuse a scrap of the appliqué fabric before you begin because fusing is not suit-

able for all fabrics, especially heat sensitive fabrics.

Cut the fusible web the same size, or slightly smaller than, the appliqué pieces (A). Sandwich the web between the appliqué (right side up) and the background fabric. Fuse in place, following the manufacturer's directions for the fusible web. The bond created by the fusing keeps the appliqué from pulling away from the fabric in the unstitched area after repeated washings.

A

If your background fabric won't feed smoothly through the machine, or if it is so lightweight that it keeps getting swallowed up in the throat plate opening, put a piece of nonwoven, tear-away stabilizing material, such as Stitch-n-Tear™ or Trace Erase™, between the feed dogs and your fabric as you sew.

Fabric Glue Stick: Use this method as an alternative to fusing or on any fabric that cannot be successfully fused in place. Working on the wrong side of the fabric, apply a thin layer of the glue over the entire surface of the appliqué (B). With right side up, press the appliqué into position with your fingers. Be sure to let the glue dry for a few minutes before machine stitching or you'll end up with a gummy needle.

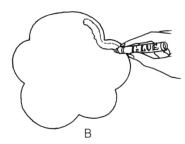

B

Stitching the Appliqué Once the appliqué is securely basted in place, it is attached to the garment with a narrow to medium width zigzag stitch. Use a very short stitch length to produce a smooth, even satin stitch effect. In general, the smaller the appliqué and/or the more curves it has, the narrower your zigzag stitch should be.

Position your garment so that the appliqué is just to the left of the needle when the needle is in the far right-hand position.

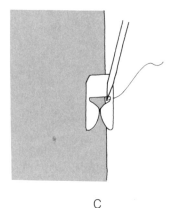

C

Hold the needle thread taut and to the back of the presser foot as you begin your stitching. As you stitch, the right swing of the needle should go into the background fabric right next to the appliqué edge (C). Stitch s-l-o-w-l-y. It's the key to smooth edges and good control. When your stitches need to meet, or end at, a previous row of satin stitches, finish stitching as close as possible to the first stitches. Remove the project from the machine and pull the thread ends to the wrong side. Tie them off and trim them close to the knot.

Corners: Pivoting is the key to crisp, clean corners. To pivot, stop stitching with the needle still inserted in the fabric, raise the presser foot and turn the fabric. Lower the presser foot and continue stitching.

If your sewing machine has a specially designed satin stitch foot or embroidery foot, use it to attach appliqués. The wide channel on the underside of the foot, just behind the needle hole, allows the foot to move smoothly over the satin stitches without flattening them.

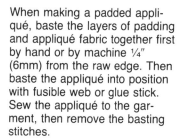

For outside corners, stitch all the way to the end of the appliqué edge. Stop with the needle inserted in the fabric at the far right-hand position. Pivot the fabric and continue stitching along the next edge of the appliqué (D).

ing with the needle inserted in the appliqué at the far left-hand position. Swivel the fabric slightly and continue stitching (G).

When making a padded appliqué, baste the layers of padding and appliqué fabric together first by hand or by machine ¼" (6mm) from the raw edge. Then baste the appliqué into position with fusible web or glue stick. Sew the appliqué to the garment, then remove the basting stitches.

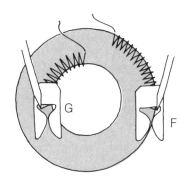

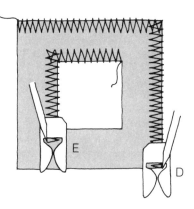

For inside corners, stitch past the corner, into the appliqué, for a distance equal to the width of your zigzag stitch. Stop with the needle inserted into the appliqué at the far left-hand position. Pivot the fabric and continue stitching along the next edge of the appliqué (E).

Curves: Smooth curves rely on the swiveling technique that follows. Move the fabric to avoid having the needle go too far off the edge of the appliqué curve. Deeper curves require that you stop and swivel at more frequent intervals than shallow curves.

For outside curves, stop stitching with the needle inserted into the background fabric at the far right-hand position. Swivel the fabric slightly and continue stitching (F).

For inside curves, stop stitch-

Points: Stitch until the needle goes off the appliqué edge in the left-hand position. Pivot the fabric slightly so that the point is centered under the presser foot. Decrease the stitch width so that the stitching continues to go across the point and just into the background fabric on both sides of the appliqué. Sew one stitch at a time, continuing to decrease the stitch width until it is at or near zero, to form the point. Pivot the fabric and stitch up the other side of the point, gradually increasing the stitch width until you return to the original size stitch (H).

Treat the points of your appliqué with a dot of liquid seam finish, such as Fray Check™, before fusing or glue basting them in place. This helps keep the points from raveling as you zigzag over them.

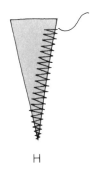

Use transfer web to painlessly attach embroidered insignias and appliqués, especially those with many cutouts or small edges.

1. Place the appliqué face down on a scrap of brown paper.

2. Cut a piece of web and backing material that is slightly larger than the appliqué. Place it web side down over the appliqué. Following the manufacturer's directions, transfer the web to the appliqué.

3. Remove the release sheet or peel the paper backing away, then remove the appliqué from the brown paper. All the excess web will adhere to the paper.

4. Fuse the appliqué to the garment according to the manufacturer's directions.

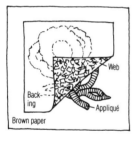

NO-SEW APPLICATION

Create your own iron-on patches from the fabric of your choice by using one of the special transfer webs, such as Transfuse™ or Wonder-Under™. They have either a paper backing or a separate wax-paperlike release sheet. The heat of your iron transfers the web to the back of your fabric, creating your own fusible fabric. Test the transfer first on a scrap of appliqué fabric and your fashion fabric.

1. Using your iron and following the manufacturer's directions, transfer the web to a piece of fabric slightly larger than the appliqué, then remove the release sheet (A).

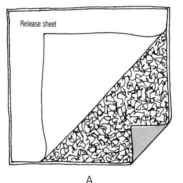

A

2. Trace the appliqué design onto the fabric and cut out the shape (B).

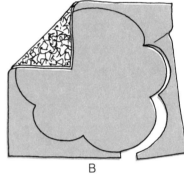

B

3. Fuse the appliqué in place on your fashion fabric, following the manufacturer's directions.

For more information:

see FUSIBLE WEB.

on Patches, see under REPAIRS.

Bands

A neckline band provides an opening large enough for the child to get a garment over his or her head, which makes it easy for children to dress themselves.

MOCK BAND

This technique creates the illusion of a band on any finished edge. Use it around a faced neckline, at the opening of a slit neckline, down both sides of a center front opening, even around the lower edge of a sleeve.

Measure and mark ¾" to 1" (20mm to 2.5cm) from the finished edge. Then topstitch along the marking, catching the facing underneath.

DIRECT BAND APPLICATION

This is an easy way to apply neckbands and wristbands made of ribbing or self-fabric.

To apply the band, use either the stretch stitch on your conventional sewing machine or the three- or three / four - thread overlock stitch on an overlock machine.

1. Cut out the band according to your pattern instructions.

2. Stitch the band together to form a circle.

3. For a neckband, stitch the garment together at the shoulder seams. For a wristband, stitch the sleeve underarm seam.

4. Divide the edge of the band and the edge of the garment into quarters. Mark these quarter points with pins or an erasable marking pen. Pin the band to the garment edge at the opening, matching all marking points. Working with the ribbing or band side up, stitch around the opening. When applying a band made from ribbing, stretch the ribbing to fit by gently pulling on it in front of the needle as you sew. For self-fabric bands, do not stretch as you sew, or stretch only slightly, depending on the type of fabric and where you're applying the band.

Here's how to combine the direct band application method with the Flat Construction Method when sewing a neckband or wristband:

1. Sew one shoulder or the sleeve underarm seam.

2. Attach the ribbing or band as mentioned previously.

3. Sew the other shoulder or sleeve seam, stitching from the armhole or wrist edge to the end of the band.

For more information:

on Pivoting, see under APPLIQUÉ.

see FLAT CONSTRUCTION METHOD.

see INTERFACING.

on Edgestitching, Reinforcement Stitching and Topstitching, see under MACHINE STITCHING.

see OVERLOCK STITCHING.

on Clipping, Grading and Trimming, see under SEAMS.

on Transferring Markings, see under WHAT TO KNOW BEFORE YOU SEW.

Basting

Everyone who sews has been tempted, at one time or another, to regard basting as one of those "why bother?" procedures. But a little time spent basting is good insurance against a lot of time spent ripping out a poorly stitched seam. Fortunately for today's sewer, there are other choices besides hand basting.

PIN BASTING

To pin baste, begin by matching and pinning the garment sections together at all matching points such as notches and symbols. Place additional pins 1" to 4" (2.5 to 10cm) apart and perpendicular to the seamline. Closely space pins at curves and corners to keep the fabric from slipping as it is turned or pivoted. Slippery or hard-to-handle fabrics require more frequent pinning than fabrics that do not shift or slide during sewing.

Don't sew over the pins! They can break your sewing machine needle. Slow down just before you reach each pin and remove it.

MACHINE BASTING

Machine basting is used to temporarily hold the fabric together at times when pin basting isn't secure enough. For example, if you want to check the fit of the garment before permanently stitching it together, machine basting is the best method.

Pin baste the garment sections together first. Then set your machine at the longest stitch length, up to ¼" (6mm), and stitch, removing each pin as you reach it. When you finish stitching, clip the bobbin thread approximately every inch (2.5cm) so that the basting stitches can be easily removed once the permanent stitching is completed.

Put an end to pins in the carpet and pins on the floor.

■ Attach a self-stick strip of magnetic material next to the throat plate of your machine to "park" pins as you remove them.

■ "Sweep" the floor with Grab-bit®, a hard plastic pincushion-sized saucer with a powerful magnet. It can find pins in the carpet before bare feet do.

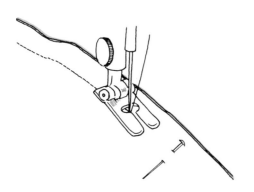

BASTING TAPE

Basting tape is a double-faced adhesive tape. It can be used almost anywhere in the garment as long as you don't stitch through the tape, and you can remove it once the stitching is completed. Basting tape is invaluable when sewing on hard-to-handle fabrics, those that require precise matching or those that cannot be pin-basted.

Place the tape ¼" (6mm) from the stitching line, on the seam allowance. Peel off the backing paper. Machine stitch, then remove the tape immediately so it won't get caught in other seams or stitches. If it does, it will be almost impossible to remove.

To use the tape, cut it to the desired length, then place it, sticky side down, on the area to be basted. Peel off the backing paper and position the taped section on the other layer of fabric. For best results, place the tape next to, but not on, the stitching line on the seam allowance. After stitching, remove the tape by peeling it off or by soaking or washing the garment section in warm water.

GLUE STICK BASTING

Glue stick basting is a fast, easy way to hold seams, trims, pockets, appliqués, facings or zippers in place before stitching. It works best on firmly woven or

Press them together with your fingers and let them dry for a few minutes before stitching.

NO BASTING

If speedy sewing is one of your goals, you can learn to sew some areas of your garment with little or no basting. You cannot use this technique on slippery or stretchy fabrics, or on seams where a lot of easing is necessary. It also does not work well when you are sewing several layers of fabric together.

Align the top edges and match any markings on your fabric. The first few times you attempt this technique, you might want to pin baste at a few points. As you

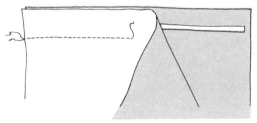

DISAPPEARING BASTING TAPE

Disappearing basting tape is a clear, double-faced adhesive tape that dissolves when the garment is washed so you can stitch right over it. Don't press over it until it has been removed. Because the adhesive dissolves in water, but not in dry-cleaning solvent, don't use it with dry-clean-only fabrics.

knitted fabrics that don't slip, ripple or have a deep pile. Glue sticks are formulated to wash out completely; however, it's a good idea to glue and wash a sample of your fabric before applying the glue stick to your garment sections.

Apply the glue stick lightly along the sections to be basted.

Remove any basting stitches as soon as you have permanently stitched that seam before they become difficult to remove.

If your sewing machine has an even feed or a walking foot, use it when you are sewing without any basting. These attachments are designed to help prevent puckering and shifting of fabric layers as you sew.

guide the fabric under the presser foot, put your left hand behind it and your right hand in front. Keep the two layers even at the edges as you sew. With practice, you should be able to eliminate the pins completely.

HAND BASTING

Although hand basting is the slowest of all the basting techniques, there are times when it is the very best method to use. Use it in areas that require a great deal of easing and on curves and sharp corners that might not align perfectly if other basting methods were used. Sometimes, detail areas such as pleats, plackets and welt pockets are much easier to make accurately if you hand baste the pieces together first. See page 107 for information on how to baste by hand.

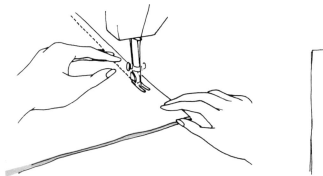

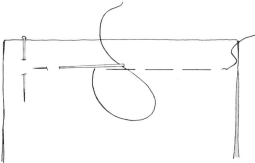

Belts

Children's patterns may include simple-to-sew belts. Folded-and-stitched tie belts and ribbon sashes are the easiest choices.

FOLDED-AND-STITCHED BELT

Patterns that feature tie belts include the pattern pieces and the directions. If you don't have a pattern, there's a simple way to determine the best length for the belt and the amount of fabric needed.

To determine the length, wrap a piece of string or ribbon around the child's waist. Tie it the way you plan to tie the finished belt and decide how long you want the ends to be. Add 1¼" (3.2cm) for the seam allowances at each end.

To determine the width, decide how wide you want the finished belt to be, double that measurement and add 1¼" (3.2cm) for the seam allowances on both long edges.

Using these two measurements, cut out the tie belt along the lengthwise grain of the fabric wherever possible.

1. *Press all four edges ⅝" (15mm) to the wrong side, pressing the long sides under first.*

2. *If your fabric is bulky, you'll need to trim away the excess at the corners and miter them. To do this, open out the fabric at each corner, refold it diagonally*

and trim as shown (A). Refold the sides and ends. They should meet at the corners, but not overlap (B).

3. *With wrong sides together, fold the belt in half lengthwise, matching the folded edges. Pin*

baste along the edges (C). Press the crease in at the foldline.

4. *Edgestitch the belt, through all layers (D). To keep the belt from twisting as you stitch, hold it gently in front of and behind the presser foot.*

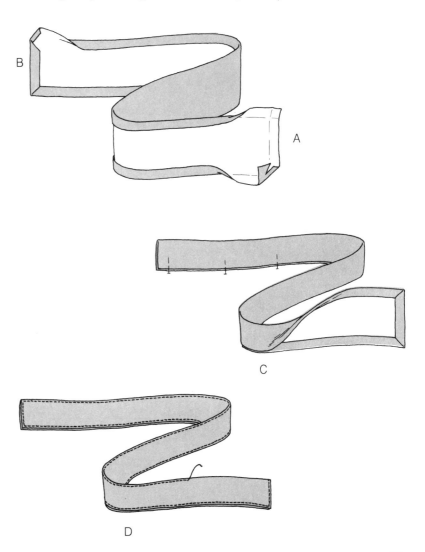

For a special touch, make a custom-coordinated belt on the overlock machine. Using thread that matches the color(s) of your fabric, stitch over lengths of narrow ribbon, braid or yarn. Braid several of these lengths together to form a belt, knotting the ends to secure them.

RIBBON SASH

To add a ribbon sash to a child's garment, you can simply purchase a few yards of ribbon, following the preceding Folded-and-Stitched Belt directions to figure the length. Wrap the ribbon around the child's waist, tie it and trim the ends diagonally to the desired length. If the ribbon ravels, machine hem the ends or seal them with Fray Check.

For more information:

on Pin Basting, see under BASTING.

on Machine-Stitched Hems, see under HEMS.

on Edgestitching, see under MACHINE STITCHING.

see OVERLOCK STITCHING.

If you are working with a fabric that is loosely woven or ravels easily, seal the edge of the trimmed corner with a bit of a seam sealant, such as Fray Check, before refolding it.

Belt Carriers

Because most children, even in their best party clothes, tend to be very active, secure and sturdy belt carriers are a real necessity.

Because the carriers should be positioned so that the belt is supported evenly and does not droop, center front and/or center back carriers are sometimes needed. To make sure the carriers are positioned evenly around the garment, measure and mark equal distances above and below the waistline seam or at the top and bottom of a waistband.

Because children's bodies lack waistline definition, there is little or no indentation at the waistline where a belt can "settle in." As a result, at least three belt carriers are required—one at each of the side seams and one at the center back of the garment. If you are making a garment with a sash that ties in the front, the weight of the tie may cause the sash to sag. To prevent this, add a fourth carrier, positioned so that it will be hidden under the bow or knot of the sash.

FABRIC BELT CARRIERS

These self-fabric carriers give a tailored look to children's cloth-ing. To prepare the fabric carriers:

1. *Determine the length of each belt carrier by measuring the width of the belt and doubling it. Then add ¼" to ½" (6 to 13mm), depending on the thickness of both the belt fabric and the carrier fabric. If the fabrics are thick, you'll need to make the carriers a little longer so that the belt can slide through easily.*

2. *Determine the total length needed for all carrier loops by multiplying the length of each finished loop by the number of loops.*

3. *Cut one long, straight strip of fabric the total length needed for all the loops. To determine how wide this strip should be, decide how wide you want the finished carriers to be and multiply by three. Cut this strip along the selvage edge of your fabric so that the belt carrier will have a prefinished edge.*

Substitute fusing for stitching when making belt carriers. Fold the fabric strip in thirds by folding the long raw edge first, then folding the selvage edge over on top. Press. Insert a strip of fusible web between the selvage layer and the raw edge. Fuse in place, following the manufacturer's directions. Cut the strip into individual carriers and you're ready to attach them to the garment.

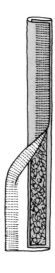

Folded-and-Stitched Carriers

1. *Prepare the carriers by measuring and cutting them out as described previously.*

2. *Fold the fabric strip in thirds by folding the long raw edge first, then folding the selvage edge over on top. Press. Edgestitch both long edges in place (A), then cut the strip into individual carriers.*

3. *Bring the ends of each carrier together and overcast them to-gether by hand. If the edges tend to fray, seal them first with a little bit of Fray Check. Position the carrier with the joined ends centered against the garment. Sew the carrier to the garment at both ends of the loop, following your pattern instructions for positioning and attaching the loops (B).*

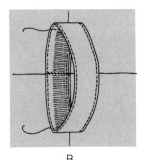

B

To make quick and easy belt carriers on the overlock machine, cut a strip of fabric three times the width of the finished carrier. Fold the strip in half lengthwise. Measuring between the fold and the cut edge, use tailor's chalk or an evaporating marking pen to make two marks indicating the width of the carrier. Position the carrier on the machine so it trims the carrier to the desired width, and stitch along each edge.

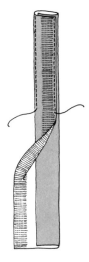

A

For more information:

see FUSIBLE WEB and OVERLOCK STITCHING.

on Overcasting, see under HAND SEWING.

on Edgestitching, see under MACHINE STITCHING.

Bindings

Bias tapes and foldover braids are stretchy items which can be used to add both a practical and a decorative touch to children's clothes. When they are used as a binding, an attractive way to finish edges, they are flexible enough to be shaped to conform to the curves of the garment.

TYPES

Prefolded bias tape, in two different styles, is available in packages and by the yard:

▶ *Single-fold bias tape is a strip of bias fabric with raw edges folded to the wrong side so they meet in the center (A). The most common width for single-fold bias tape is ½" (13mm). When it is packaged as "Wide Bias Tape," it is usually about 1" (2.5cm) wide.*

▶ *Double-fold bias tape is made the same way as single-fold tape; then an extra, slightly off-center fold is added (B). Double-fold bias tape is usually packaged in ¼" (6mm) widths. "Extra Wide" (½" or 13mm) and "Double-Fold Quilt Binding" (⅞" or 22mm) widths are also available.*

Seamlines in individual bias tape strips should be placed so they are inconspicuous on the garment.

Foldover braid is a continuous strip of woven or knitted trim that has finished edges and is folded in half lengthwise (C).

Double-fold bias tapes and foldover braids are folded slightly off center. When sewing the braid or tape to the garment, the wider side goes underneath the layers of fabric and the narrower side goes on the top. You edgestitch along the top of the braid or tape and both sides are attached in one stitching operation.

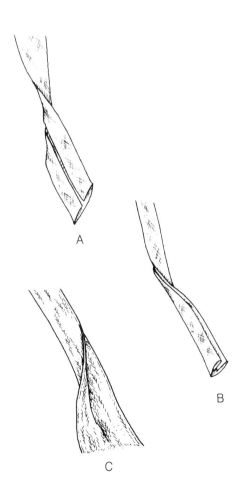

A

B

C

It's a good idea to preshrink the tape before you use it, even if it's labeled "preshrunk." With packaged tapes, remove the wrapping but leave the tape on the card. Immerse the tape, cardboard and all, in hot water for a few minutes. Take it out, bend the card slightly, let the tape dry, then remove it from the cardboard.

PRESHAPING

Before applying the tape or braid, preshape it to match the contours of the garment. Use steam, stretch the binding or braid slightly, and press lightly to shrink out any excess fullness that might cause tucks or puckers later on. As you press, make sure that the curve of the single-folded edge corresponds to the outer edge of your project and that the width of the braid stays even.

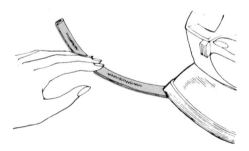

BINDING EDGES

Bias tapes and foldover braids can be used to attractively finish any outer edge of a garment. They're most frequently used to bind the edges of a reversible garment, such as a quilted vest, or to trim and finish off a neckline or armhole opening.

Your pattern may already call for bound edges. If it does not, you can eliminate the facings and then add the bias as a design detail. Begin by trimming away the seam allowances of the raw edge(s) you want to bind.

To bind straight and curved edges, encase the garment edge with double-fold bias tape or foldover braid. Leave about 2" (5cm) of extra binding free at each end of the stitching to al-

For more information:

on Slipstitching, see under HAND SEWING.

on Backstitching and Edge-stitching, see under MACHINE STITCHING.

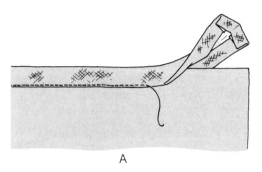

A

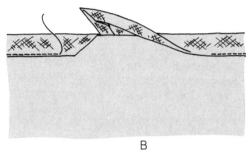

B

low for finishing. Then position the fold of the binding along the cut edge of the garment, placing the narrower side of the tape on the right side of the garment. Turn the ends under and trim them to ¼" (6mm). Pin in place as needed. Edgestitch from the right side through all layers (A). Where the binding ends meet, open out the fold, turn the raw edges under and trim them to ¼" (6mm). Refold, cover the raw edge of the garment and stitch (B). Slipstitch the joining.

BINDING CORNERS

1. *To bind outer square corners without a pucker, pin and edgestitch the tape or braid in place through all layers until you reach the corner edge of the garment (C). Remove the garment from the machine and clip, then knot, the threads.*

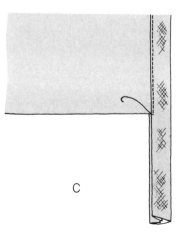

C

2. *Turn the tape around the corner and pin in place (D). Miter the corner by making a diagonal fold in the tape at the corner, both on top and underneath. Press, then pin in place.*

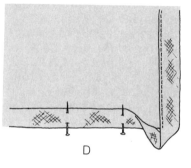

D

3. *Beginning just below the diagonal fold, backstitch, then edgestitch down the remaining edge of the tape (E). If the tape or braid does not lie flat at the corners, secure the mitered fold by slipstitching in place.*

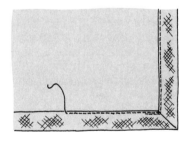

E

Buttons and Buttonholes

When selecting buttons for children's clothes, some special considerations are in order. Buttons should be washable, unless they are for a seldom-worn party dress. Buttons should be sturdy—children's clothes are not the place for delicate porcelain buttons or other fragile fasteners. Buttons on babies' and toddlers' garments should be sewn on extra securely—these are the stages of childhood when everything goes into their mouths! Large buttons with smooth, easy-to-grasp shapes are useful for toddlers who are learning to dress themselves.

ATTACHING BUTTONS BY HAND

Sew-through buttons can be sewn on by hand or by machine (consult your machine manual for the proper procedure). Shank buttons, however, can only be attached by hand because there is no way to reach the hole in the base of the shank with your sewing machine.

Hand sewing a button on can be a portable project. Do it while you are watching television, talking on the phone or waiting for an appointment.

Your sewing will go faster if you use a double strand of thread, about 18" (46cm) long. If the thread tends to twist or knot, pull it through beeswax before you begin. For extra strength, use heavy-duty or button-and-carpet thread. To attach a sew-through button by hand:

1. Secure your stitching at the beginning by taking a few backstitches right at the marking for the button placement.

2. Insert the needle up through one of the holes, then down through another hole and into the fabric. Repeat, going back and forth through the holes three or four more times until the button is secured. The completed stitches should be parallel to each other, not crisscrossing.

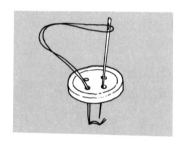

3. If you want a thread shank, place a toothpick on top of the button and sew over it as you go back and forth between the holes. Once the button is secured, wind the threads firmly around the stitches several times to form the shank.

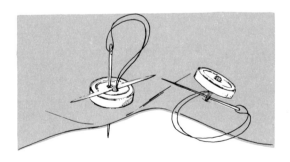

4. Insert the needle through the fabric to the underside of the garment and tack securely.

To attach a shank button by hand:

1. Secure your stitching at the beginning by taking a few backstitches right at the marking for the button placement.

2. Align the wider part of the button shank with the direction of your buttonhole marking. This will be either vertical or horizontal, as indicated on your pattern tissue.

3. Sew through the shank, then through the fabric. Repeat three or four times.

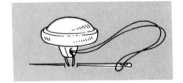

For tiny fingers that like to dress themselves, save small, shaped buttons for decoration only or use bits of Velcro® as the "real" closings and sew the small buttons on top.

Use elastic thread for sewing buttons on toddlers' clothes. That little extra give makes it easier for them to dress themselves.

4. *Insert the needle through the fabric to the underside of the garment and tack securely.*

5. *If your fabric is very thick or bulky, you may need to make a thread shank in addition to your built-in button shank. Follow the method described previously for attaching a sew-through button by hand, inserting a toothpick, needle or match between the base of the shank and the garment.*

MACHINE-MADE BUTTONHOLES

Buttonhole attachments and/or zigzag stitch methods vary from machine to machine. Follow the instructions for your sewing machine to practice making a few buttonholes. Your practice sample should consist of the same layers as the buttonhole area on the garment—fabric, interfacing and fabric. When you are pleased with the size and uniformity of your practice buttonholes, you are ready to make them on your garment.

Buttonhole placement is indicated on the pattern tissue by the buttonhole placement line. This placement line is positioned so that, when the garment is buttoned, the two halves will overlap and match at the center line. Horizontal buttonholes, which extend ⅛" (3mm) beyond the placement line, are marked with a horizontal line. This type of buttonhole is the most common for children's wear because it has the most give (important for active children!) and the least gap when the garment is worn. Vertical buttonholes, used most often on narrow plackets or bands, are positioned directly on the placement line, starting ⅛" (3mm) above the button marking.

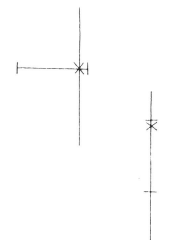

If you accidentally cut too far into the stitches of the buttonhole, use a drop of Fray Check at the corners to help repair the damage and restitch the end by machine.

To save time, stitch one buttonhole and go directly to the next one without cutting threads until the last buttonhole is stitched. Then cut the threads, pull them to the wrong side and tie in a square knot.

For more information:

on Backstitching and Tacking, see under HAND SEWING.

on Zigzag Stitching, see under MACHINE STITCHING.

on Transferring Markings, see under WHAT TO KNOW BEFORE YOU SEW.

1. *Because buttonholes are sewn on the right side of the fabric, buttonhole markings have to be transferred to the right side. Use water soluble dressmaker's carbon, water soluble or evaporating marking pens (pretested on a scrap of your fabric), tailor's chalk or transparent tape. To use tape, cut two pieces and place them on the garment about ¼" (6mm) apart so that the buttonhole stitching will fall in between the tape markings. Mark the exact buttonhole length on both pieces of tape. If your sewing machine does not stitch buttonholes automatically, the tape serves as a stitching guide, providing you with perfectly parallel lines.*

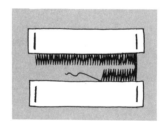

2. *Once the buttonhole is stitched, cut it open, using buttonhole scissors or small, very sharp scissors. Put a straight pin at each end of the buttonhole before you cut to keep the scissors from slicing through the stitches, then cut carefully through all the fabric layers.*

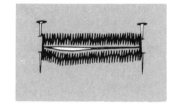

There are many times in your life when you may want to sew for children—as a new mother, a friend making a gift for another special, small friend, or a doting grandmother sewing for your grandchildren. Whenever you sew for children, you can find patterns and fabrics suitable for any event in a child's life, from the everyday occurrences of school, play and sleep to the special ones like birthday parties, christenings, first communions, confirmations, or even as a member of the wedding party.

As you explore the dynamic world of sewing for children, always keep the child's comfort foremost in your mind. Whether you make garments that are casual or elegant, conservatively trimmed or decorated with a touch of whimsy, this book can help you create clothes that you enjoy sewing and the child loves wearing.

The colorful pages that follow are meant to provide inspiration for selecting styles, fabrics, colors and trims to fit the needs of children of all ages, sizes and personalities.

Bright bands of bias tape are a quick and easy way to add cheerful accents to practical playwear.

Construction paper cutouts and coloring book motifs inspire crayon-bright appliqué designs. A closely spaced machine zigzag stitch keeps the edges secure.

Ruth Scharf Ltd.

Older children particularly enjoy play clothes with crisp, clean lines in sophisticated colorings. Cut plaids on the bias to eliminate tedious matching in small detail areas such as pockets.

J. G. Hook

A young miss and her best friend can enjoy look-alike dressing in easy-comfort knits. Styled-for-action details include drawstring waistlines, elasticized wrists and cuffs, raglan sleeves or extended shoulders.

Ruth Scharf Ltd.

Bias bindings provide an edge finish and a decorative touch to almost any child's garment on almost any type of fabric, from velveteen to cotton cord.

Always popular for schooltime wear: the classic shirtwaist dress, the easy-wear jumper and two-piece separates in classic colors.

Ruth Scharf Ltd.

Give back-to-school tartans a fresh
interpretation with a contrast collar,
delicately edged in lace and enhanced with a
black satin bow. A gray flannel jumper
wrapped in a tartan shawl imparts some
more traditional appeal.

All suited up for Sundays: a double-breasted, box jacket topping precision pleats or trouser-styled short pants. Careful pressing is the key to precision tailoring.

Everyone loves the Sunday best look of a princess-seamed coat with velvet touches. Children's coats and jackets are a wonderful way to start small as you expand your tailoring expertise.

Pinafores plus! A look that never goes out of style. You can keep them sundress-simple with just a hint of rickrack or lace or make them party-fancy with ribbons and flounces.

Narrow ribbon, used singly or in rows, can enhance the design lines of any garment. Loop several colors together for a simple, but effective, sash.

Careful attention to details results in pockets that match, corners that are precise and a garment that is a pleasure to behold.

Birthday parties are childhood happenings with magical memories. The fabrics need not be elaborate; it's the details with a handcrafted look, like smocking and lace edging, that count.

Victorian frills and wallpaper prints provide the party air. Keep everything—from the size of the print to the width of the trim—in pleasing proportion to the child's size.

Every little girl remembers that special dress that made her feel like a princess. Weddings and holidays are the time to indulge in fabrics too precious for everyday wear.

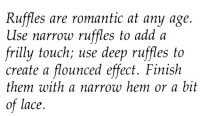

Ruffles are romantic at any age.
Use narrow ruffles to add a
frilly touch; use deep ruffles to
create a flounced effect. Finish
them with a narrow hem or a bit
of lace.

For that very special once-in-a-lifetime event, you might want to learn a traditional technique, like narrow pin tucking, or try out an easy tip, like using rows of lace to create a tucked effect. Whatever your pleasure, with children's clothes you can experiment in small amounts because the pieces are smaller than for adults' fashions.

Create a family heirloom. Delicate tucking and white-on-white embroidery ensure that this littlest fashion plate will be the best-dressed person in the room.

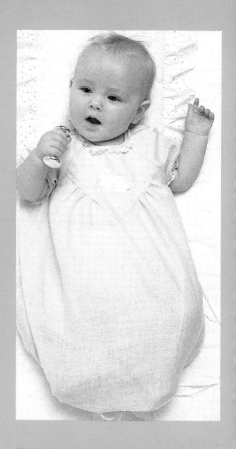

Sleepyheads of all ages love soft, brushed fabrics. Look for easy-care fabrics that can withstand the frequent washings that sleepwear demands.

Casings

Casings are a popular detail on children's clothes because they are a comfortable, unrestricting way to control fullness. You'll find them at necklines, waistlines and sleeve edges. On infants' and toddlers' clothes, casings are often used around the leg openings of panties and rompers.

Your pattern tissue includes casing markings that should be transferred to the wrong side of the fabric. There are two basic types of casings—applied and folded. Both are tunnels of fabric that encase a drawstring or an elastic.

APPLIED CASINGS

For an applied casing, the tunnel is a separate strip of fabric or single-fold bias tape stitched to the garment. Make sure the casing material is slightly wider than the elastic or drawstring, or you'll have trouble pulling the inserted item through the casing. If you are using a strip of fabric, cut it the width of the elastic plus ¾" (20mm). Fold each long edge ¼" (6mm) to the wrong side and press. Purchased bias tape is prefolded, ready to use.

Off-the-Edge Casings When an applied casing is attached anywhere away from the edge of a garment, such as at the waistline of a one-piece dress, it's referred to as an **off-the-edge casing.**

1. *Pin the bias tape or fabric strip to the garment section along the placement lines indicated on your pattern tissue. Turn the short ends under so they meet but don't overlap.*

2. *Edgestitch both long edges of the casing. Insert the elastic where the ends meet and fasten the ends together with a safety pin. Then try the garment on the child and adjust the elastic to fit. Secure the ends of the elastic by sewing them together in a ½" (13mm) seam, stitching back and forth over the elastic several times. Slipstitch the opening closed.*

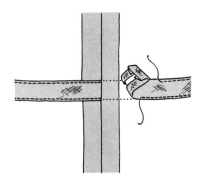

To keep them from blocking or catching the elastic or drawstring as you pull it through the finished casing, machine baste or fuse the seam allowances to the garment within the casing area before you make the casing.

On-the-Edge Casings When an applied casing is attached to the edge of a garment, such as a neckline, waistline, leg or sleeve edge, it's referred to as an **on-the-edge casing.**

1. *To prepare the fabric strip, open out the fold on one long edge of your fabric or bias tape. If you are applying a bias strip to a curved edge of the garment, use steam, stretch the strip slightly and press lightly to shrink out any fullness while preshaping the curve. With right sides together, pin the casing to the garment edge, placing the creaseline of the tape along the seamline. Turn under the ends so they meet without overlapping (A).*

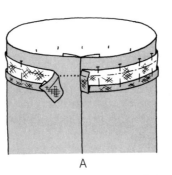

A

2. *Stitch along the crease of the casing. Trim the seam allowance even with the edge of the casing (B). Press the casing away from the garment.*

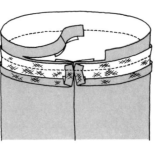

B

3. *Fold the casing to the inside of the garment, making sure it doesn't peek out at the garment edge. Press the fold toward the garment, then edgestitch the casing to the garment along the folded edge (C). If the pattern calls for elastic, insert it in the opening and pull it through. Fasten the ends together with a safety pin. Then try the garment on the child and adjust the elastic to fit. Secure the ends of the elastic by sewing them together in a ½" (13mm) seam, stitching back and forth over the elastic several times. Slipstitch the opening closed (D).*

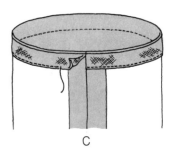

C

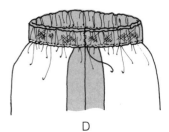

D

FOLDED CASINGS

To create a folded casing, the edge of the garment is extended so that it can be turned to the inside and stitched in place. If you are making a casing for a drawstring, remember that the drawstring should be slightly narrower than the casing so it can be pulled through easily.

1. *Turn the raw edge under ¼" (6mm) and press. Then fold the garment extension to the wrong side along the casing foldline and press again (A).*

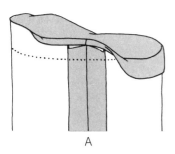

A

2. *Edgestitch the turned-under raw edge to form the casing. To provide an opening to insert the elastic, begin and end stitching at either side of a seamline (B).*

To prevent the elastic from twisting or rolling as the child wears the garment, edgestitch the casing along the folded edge of the garment (C).

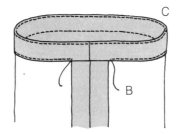

C

B

3. *Insert, adjust and secure elastic, following step 3 of On-the-Edge Casings, above. Edgestitch the casing opening closed. As you edgestitch, carefully align the new stitches with the previous stitches (D).*

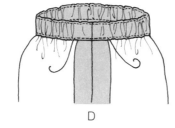

D

For more information:

on Machine Basting, see under BASTING.

on Preshaping Binding and Single-fold Bias Tape, see under BINDING.

see DRAWSTRINGS.

see ELASTIC.

see FUSIBLE WEB.

on Slipstitching, see under HAND SEWING.

on Edgestitching, see under MACHINE STITCHING.

on Transferring Markings, see under WHAT TO KNOW BEFORE YOU SEW.

Collars

Although there are many different styles of collars—sailor; shawl; stand-up, such as the mandarin; and flat collars, such as the Peter Pan—they are all constructed using the same basic techniques because nearly every collar has a corner or a curve.

MAKING COLLARS

Collars are generally assembled in the following order:

1. *Apply the interfacing to one collar section (see pages 118–21).*

2. *Sew the upper collar and the under collar together.*

3. *Trim and grade the seam allowances.*

4. *Notch the curves or clip the corners.*

5. *Turn and press the collar.*

6. *Attach the collar to the garment.*

SANDWICH COLLAR APPLICATION

In this method, the collar is attached to the garment by inserting it between the garment and the neckline facing. Before attaching the collar, staystitch the neckline edges of the garment and the facing to prevent them from stretching out of shape.

1. *Clip the garment along the neck edge just to, but not through, the staystitching at regular intervals. With the right side of the under collar next to the right side of the garment, pin the collar in place along the garment neckline, matching all notches and symbols. If the collar doesn't seem to fit between any of the matching points,* make additional clips in the garment neck edge. Then machine baste the collar in place (A).

2. *Stitch the front and back facings together at the shoulder seams, then finish the long, unnotched edge of the facing. Clip the facing along the neck edge just to, but not through, the staystitching at regular intervals. Place the facing on top of the collar, right sides together, matching the neckline edges of all the layers and all construction symbols. Pin baste or machine baste the facing in place (B). Trim the facing shoulder seam allowances diagonally at the neck edge.*

3. *Stitch the collar to the garment (C).*

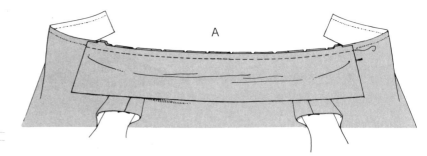

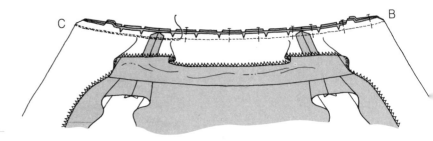

Although the understitching helps keep the facing from sticking up or rolling out, you can provide some extra insurance against that happening. Tack the facing down at each shoulder seam with a few hand stitches or a small piece of fusible web.

4. *Trim and grade the neckline seam allowances, then clip to the seamline through all layers and trim the corners of the facing (D). Turn the facing to the inside and press it away from the collar. Understitch the facing to* *keep it from rolling to the outside by stitching close to the neckline seam within 1" (2.5cm) of each end, through the facing and the neck seam allowances only (E). Do not catch the garment in your stitching.*

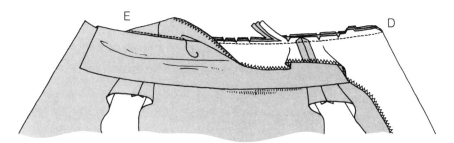

To quickly attach a convertible collar on the overlock machine, staystitch the neck edge of the collar and front facing. Then clip the seam allowance at frequent intervals until the neck edge forms a straight line and lies flat. Overlock the long, unnotched edges and shoulder areas of the facings. Pin the collar in place on the neckline, fold the facings in along the foldline, pin them over the collar and overlock the neck edge. Turn the front facings right side out and press the collar away from, and the seam allowances toward, the garment.

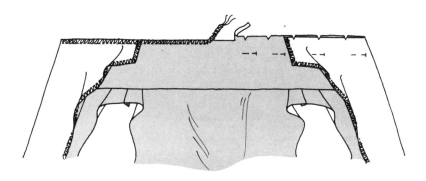

For more information:

on Machine and Pin Basting, see under BASTING.

see FUSIBLE WEB.

on Tacking, see under HAND SEWING.

on Applying Interfacing, see under INTERFACING.

on Edgestitching, Reinforcement Stitching, Staystitching, Topstitching and Understitching, see under MACHINE STITCHING.

on Clipping, Grading, Notching and Trimming, see under SEAMS AND SEAM FINISHES.

on Pressing Seams, see under WHAT TO KNOW BEFORE YOU SEW.

Cuffs

Cuffs add an extra-special finishing touch to sleeves and pants legs. Self-faced barrel or band cuffs are cut separately and then attached to the edge of the sleeve or the pants leg. These cuffs can match or contrast with the body of the garment. Keep in mind that you will have to buy additional fabric to create contrasting cuffs if your pattern does not have them.

Turnback cuffs are formed by folding the lower edge of the garment to the right side and securing it. Turnback cuffs, such as the traditional trouser cuff, always match the body of the garment.

To maintain the shape of the cuff and to give it body, interfacing is usually required, although it is sometimes omitted from the turnback cuff when a soft appearance is desired.

The outer layer of the cuff, the one with the notch, is the layer that should be interfaced with either a fusible or a sew-in interfacing. If you are using a fusible type, the interfacing should extend only to the foldline (A). If you are using a sew-in type, and the finished cuff is to be edgestitched or topstitched, the interfacing should extend only to the foldline; if it is not to be edgestitched or topstitched, the interfacing should extend ½" (13mm) beyond the foldline (B).

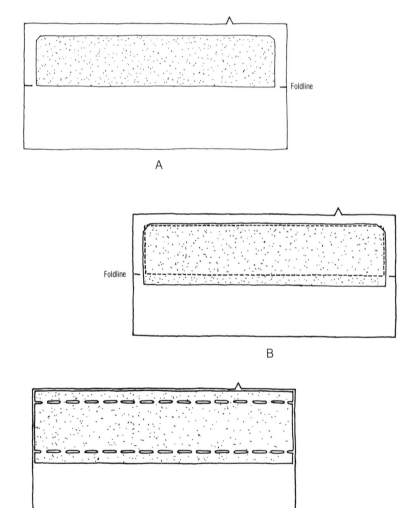

Depending on the finished width of your cuff, the special precut fusible interfacings, such as Fuse 'n Fold®, are real time-savers. Because these interfacings have perforations that are meant to be aligned with the foldlines and stitching lines, the interfacing extends beyond the foldline.

BARREL OR BAND CUFF

One of the easiest cuffs to make, the barrel or band version can be applied to a garment with or without a placket opening. If the sleeve has a placket opening, sew the sleeve underarm seam and construct the placket according to the pattern instructions before making the cuff. If the sleeve does not have a placket opening, use the Flat Construction Method and do not sew the sleeve underarm seam until the cuff has been attached, as follows:

1. *Turn under ⅝" (15mm) on the long edge of the uninterfaced section of the cuff and press. With right sides together, pin the notched edge of the cuff to the lower edge of the sleeve, matching all notches and markings. Stitch along the seamline; then trim and grade the seam allowances (A).*

2. *Press the cuff away from, and the seam allowances toward, the cuff. Sew the side and sleeve seams, from the top of the sleeve to the bottom of the cuff, in one operation, and press it open. Turn the cuff to the inside of the sleeve along the foldline. Bring the folded edge of the cuff over the seam allowances to meet the stitching line and pin or hand baste in place (B). Slipstitch or edgestitch the folded edge in place (C).*

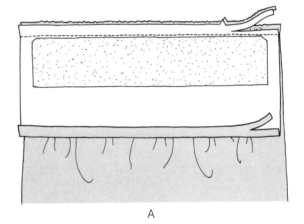

A

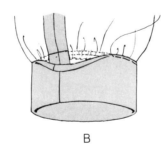

B

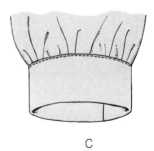

C

DIRECT BAND CUFF APPLICATION

Barrel or band cuffs can be attached to the garment by using the overcast stitch on your conventional machine, set to a short, wide stitch length, or a three- or three/four-thread overlock stitch on an overlock machine.

For a Sleeve Without an Opening:

1. Sew the sleeve underarm seam.

2. Stitch the cuff ends together along the seam to form a circle. With wrong sides together, fold the cuff along the foldline and press. Baste the raw edges of the cuff together.

3. With the right side of the sleeve to the interfaced section of the cuff, pin the sleeve and cuff together, adjusting any fullness and matching all marking points. Stitch on the seamline. If you're using a conventional sewing machine, trim away the excess seam allowance, being careful not to clip the stitches (A). The excess seam allowance will be trimmed away automatically by the overlock machine. Press the cuff away from, and the seam allowances toward, the body of the sleeve.

ing and sew the sleeve underarm seam according to your pattern instructions.

2. With right sides together, fold the cuff in half along the foldline and sew the short ends. Trim the seam allowances. Turn the cuff to the right side and press.

3. With the right side of the sleeve to the interfaced section of the cuff, pin the sleeve and cuff together, adjusting any fullness and matching all marking points. Stitch on the seamline, through all thicknesses, starting and stopping stitching at the cuff ends. Trim away the excess seam allowance if you're using a conventional sewing machine (B)— it will automatically be cut off by an overlock machine. Then turn the seam allowances to the inside and press the cuff away from, and the seam allowances toward, the body of the sleeve.

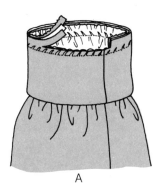

A

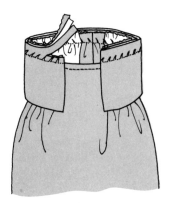

B

For a Sleeve with a Narrow Hem Opening:

1. Make the narrow hem open-

TURNBACK CUFFS

A turnback cuff is actually a deep hem which is folded to the right side of the garment. Before you begin, be sure that you have transferred the foldline and hemline markings to your garment so that they are clearly visible.

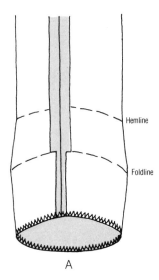

A

1. *To eliminate bulk, trim the sleeve or pants seam allowances below the foldline of the cuff. Finish the lower raw edge, using any method appropriate for your fabric (A).*

2. *Fold the cuff to the inside along the foldline. Baste close to the foldline; then machine stitch the finished edge in place (B). This hem will be invisible on the right side of the garment because it will be covered by the cuff.*

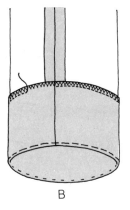

B

3. *Fold the cuff to the right side along the hemline. Tack it at the seamline(s) with a few hand stitches concealed between the layers (C).*

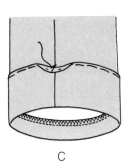

C

For more information:

see BASTING.

see FLAT CONSTRUCTION METHOD.

on Slipstitching and Tacking, see under HAND SEWING.

on Applying Interfacing, see under INTERFACING.

on Edgestitching, Overcast or Overlock Stitching, and Topstitching, see under MACHINE STITCHING.

on Finishing Seams, Grading and Trimming, see under SEAMS

on Transferring Markings, see under WHAT TO KNOW BEFORE YOU SEW.

Darts

A dart is a construction detail with two very definite functions: it helps direct and control fullness in a garment and it helps shape the garment to body contours. Because children's bodies have very few contours, darts are not as common a detail on children's clothes as on adults'. Infants' and toddlers' clothes almost never have darts. However, as the child gets older, a waistline begins to develop, so pants and skirt patterns will feature hipline darts and dress patterns, back waistline darts. Dart *tucks* may also be used to provide shape and direct fullness.

MARKING

Because darts are designed to fall precisely where they are needed, it is important to accurately transfer the markings from your pattern tissue. Transfer these markings to the wrong side of the fabric so you can see them as you sew. To make sure your finished dart has the proper contours, mark both the O's and the stitching lines.

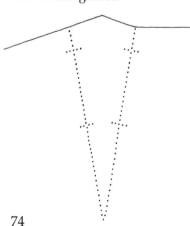

STITCHING

1. *With right sides together, fold the garment section through the center of the dart, adjusting the fold until the markings match. To be sure they are matched, insert a pin straight into the fabric at a mark on one side of the dart. It should exit at the corresponding mark on the other side of the dart. Pin baste the dart together, inserting the pins perpendicular to the stitching line (A).*

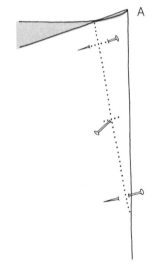

A

2. *Sew the dart from the widest end to the narrowest, tapering to nothing at the point. The last two or three stitches should be on the fold. To secure the threads at the end of the dart, tie them in a knot. Never backstitch at the tip of a dart. It's all too easy to distort the point, creating ripples and puckers.*

For more information:

on Pin Basting, see under BASTING.

on Pressing Darts and Transferring Markings, see under WHAT TO KNOW BEFORE YOU SEW.

To tie a perfect knot at a dart point, or anywhere else, loop the thread ends into a knot. Then place a straight pin through the center of the knot, resting the tip of the pin where you want the knot to end up. As you tighten the threads, the knot will automatically slide to the tip of the pin and lie flat against the fabric.

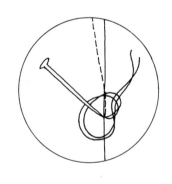

Drawstrings

In addition to offering children a handy way to learn bow tying, drawstrings provide a comfortable, adjustable way to gather in fullness. The usual locations for drawstrings are at the waistline and the neckline, around the rim of a hood and even at the lower edge of baby buntings.

The simplest drawstrings are made from cording, ribbon or strips of leather that are simply trimmed to the desired length and require no further sewing. However, drawstrings can also be made from strips or tubes of self-fabric.

The finished drawstring should be slightly narrower than the casing or casing opening so that it can be pulled through easily. Remember that the width of the finished drawstring should determine how wide the opening will be. The drawstring should be long enough to wrap around the body at the desired point and to tie a knot or a bow plus ½" (13mm) for seam allowances.

Two of the easiest drawstrings to make are the folded-and-stitched and the overlocked drawstrings. Begin by determining the length and width of the drawstring, then cut a strip of fabric the required width and length.

FOLDED-AND-STITCHED METHOD

1. *Turn each short end ¼" (6mm) to the wrong side and press; repeat for the long edges.*

2. *With wrong sides together, fold the fabric strip in half lengthwise, matching the folded edges. Press in the crease along the foldline. Edgestitch around the drawstring, through all layers. Insert the drawstring into the casing, using a bodkin or safety pin.*

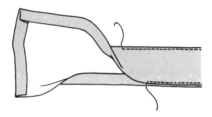

OVERLOCK METHOD

This technique works best on lightweight fabrics using the three-thread stitch on a three- or three/four-thread overlock machine.

1. *Before stitching the fabric on the machine, overlock a chain that is 6" (15cm) longer than the finished drawstring. Do not cut the chain away from the machine.*

2. *Place the chain on the right side of the fabric strip, along the lengthwise center, with approxi-*

mately 4" (10cm) of the chain extending below the lower edge of the fabric (A).

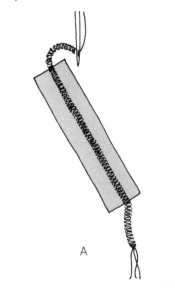

A

If you use the selvage edge of your fabric for one long edge of the drawstring, you will have one automatically finished edge. You can do this if the selvage doesn't have any markings, such as the manufacturer's name, printed along the edge. Cut the fabric slightly narrower than three times the width of the opening. After pressing the short ends ¼" (6mm) to the wrong side, fold the fabric strip in thirds. First, fold the long raw edge; then fold the selvage edge over on top. Press, then edgestitch around the drawstring, through all the layers.

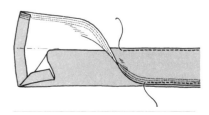

3. *Fold the fabric in half over the chain, raw edges matching, and overlock stitch (B).*

4. *Turn the drawstring right side out by gently pulling on the thread chain (C). Clip off the chain and secure the thread ends with a drop of Fray Check. To finish the drawstring, tuck the*

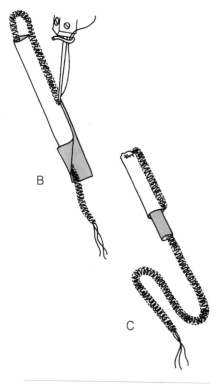

To keep the drawstring from being pulled out of the garment or from shifting out of place once it is inserted, match the center of the drawstring and casing and stitch through all the layers at this point. The drawstring can then be used to gather up both sides of the garment equally.

raw ends to the inside and slipstitch the openings closed. Insert the drawstring into the casing, using a bodkin or safety pin. If desired, tie each end in a knot.

DRAWSTRING OPENINGS

A drawstring is inserted into the casing through an opening on the *right* side of the garment. The width of the opening is determined by the finished width of the drawstring. Unless the opening occurs along the closure edges of a garment, such as at the waistline of a front zippered jacket, it is usually made *before* the casing.

Buttonhole Put a patch of fusible interfacing behind the buttonhole area to reinforce it. Then make two machine buttonholes on the outside of the garment, slightly longer than the width of the drawstring, where indicated on the pattern tissue.

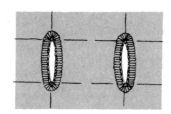

Seam Drawstring openings along a seamline are created as the seam is stitched. To reinforce the opening area, fuse small rectangles of soft interfacing to the wrong side of the fabric, along the seamline over the markings that indicate the opening (A). Then stitch the seam, leaving an opening where indicated on the pattern tissue. To secure the stitches and pro-

vide additional reinforcement, backstitch at either end of the opening (B). Press the seam open (C).

Once the opening and the casing are completed, use a bodkin or safety pin attached to the end of the drawstring to push it through one opening; then push it along the length of the casing and pull it out the other end.

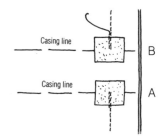

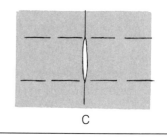

For more information:

see CASINGS.

on Machine-Made Buttonholes, see under FASTENERS.

on Slipstitching, see under HAND SEWING.

on Fusible Interfacing, see under INTERFACING.

on Backstitching and Edge-stitching, see under MACHINE STITCHING.

see OVERLOCK STITCHING.

Elastic

Elastic is a common feature just about anywhere in a child's garment—around the leg opening of short or long pants, at the lower edge of a sleeve, at the waistline of dresses, skirts and pants, even at the upper edge of a sundress or sunsuit. Elastic is particularly popular in children's wear because it makes the garment easy to get on and off and helps keep it in place throughout a day of active play.

CHOOSING THE RIGHT ELASTIC

Your pattern envelope tells you how much and what width elastic to purchase. The type and fiber content of the elastic you buy depends on where and how you intend to use it.

Types **Braided elastic** is strong and lightweight with lengthwise, parallel ribs (A). It narrows when stretched, which makes it suitable for casings but not for direct applications. Because the rubber is not completely covered in this type of elastic, the repeated stabbing action of the sewing machine needle during the direct application method pierces and breaks the rubber. This can harm the elastic so that it will no longer stretch and recover.

Woven and **knitted elastics** (B, C) feel softer than braided elastic, and are just as strong, but do not narrow when stretched. They are a good choice for casings and direct applications, particularly where the elastic comes in direct contact with a child's skin.

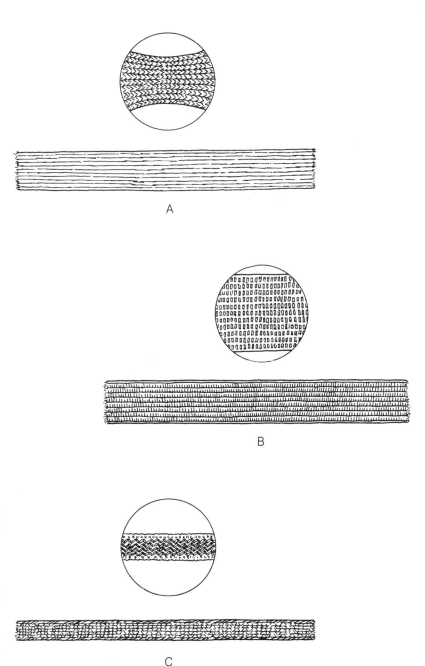

A

B

C

Mesh elastic (D) is knitted and designed for direct applications, rather than for casings. It's a good choice for the waistbands of skirts and pants.

No-roll waistband elastic (E, F) features crosswise ribs specially designed to keep it from rolling or twisting. It's a good choice for waistband casings on play clothes.

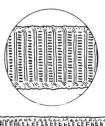

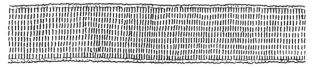

D

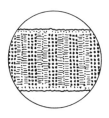

E

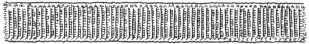

F

Fiber Content Rubber or spandex provides the stretch in all elastics. However, when other fibers are combined with rubber or spandex, different characteristics result.

Polyester elastic, which is braided, knitted or woven, can be washed or dry-cleaned. Because it is shrink resistant and unaffected by body oils, salt or chlorinated water, it is a particularly good choice for swimwear and play clothes.

Nylon elastic is similar to the polyester type. However, because some nylon elastic may turn yellow when exposed to chlorine, don't use it for swimwear or garments you may wish to clean with chlorine bleach (unless it is marked specifically for swimwear).

Rayon and **acetate elastics** stretch when they are wet and do not return to their original size until dry. Because active children often perspire heavily, these elastics are not a good choice for swimwear or for play clothes.

Cotton elastic is soft and absorbent, recovers well and stands up after many washings. It's a good choice for infants' clothing and for sleepwear.

Elastic can be applied directly to the edge of a garment or inserted into a casing.

DIRECT APPLICATION

Applying elastic directly to the edge of the fabric so that it does not twist or roll saves the time of making a casing and inserting the elastic.

Concealed Application

1. *Cut the elastic the length recommended in the pattern instructions. If you are not using the Flat Construction Method, overlap the ends and stitch them together on your machine to form a circle (A).*

2. *Trim the seam allowance of the garment edge to equal the width of the elastic (B).*

3. *Divide the elastic and the garment edge into quarters and mark with pins or a water soluble marking pen (C).*

4. *Pin the elastic to the wrong side of the garment edge, matching markings. The outer edge of the elastic should be even with the cut edge of the garment. With the elastic facing up, zigzag, overcast, straight or overlock stitch it to the edge of the garment, stretching the elastic to fit as you sew (D). If you are using an overlock machine, be careful not to cut the elastic with the knife as you overlock.*

5. *Turn the elastic and the fabric to the inside of the garment along the foldline and pin. Using either a straight or a zigzag stitch on your conventional machine, and stretching the elastic to fit as you sew, stitch again close to the cut edge of the fabric, through all the thicknesses (E).*

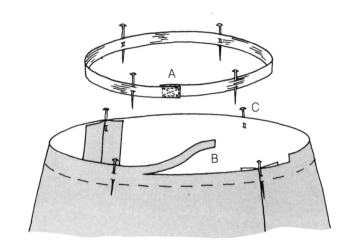

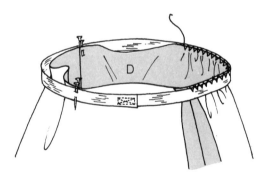

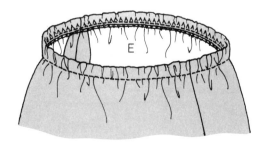

Overlock Application This application is visible on the inside and almost invisible on the outside. As you overlock, hold the elastic and the fabric firmly in place behind the needle. Stretch only the elastic (*not the fabric*) in front of the needle as you sew.

1. *Turn the garment edge to the inside along the foldline and press. Trim the seam allowance to ¼" (6mm).*

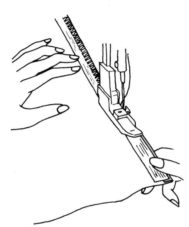

2. *Place the elastic on the wrong side of the fabric so that the outside edge of the elastic is even with the fold and pin, matching markings. Position the fabric, elastic side up, to the left of the cutting knife so that the fold is even with the throat plate. Secure the elastic with a few stitches, then overlock stitch,*

stretching the elastic to fit as you sew and being careful not to cut the elastic. Remove the pins before the cutting knife reaches them.

ELASTIC IN A CASING

Before inserting the elastic, cut it to the length specified by your pattern instructions.

1. *Attach a bodkin or safety pin to one end of the elastic and insert it into the opening in the casing. To keep the elastic from accidentally being pulled completely through the casing, use a straight pin to anchor the other end to the seam allowance at the opening. Push the bodkin or safety pin gently through the casing, working slowly so that the elastic stays flat and doesn't twist (A).*

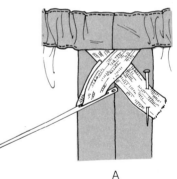

A

2. *Once the elastic is threaded completely through the casing, remove the straight pin and the bodkin or safety pin. Pin the ends of the elastic together with a safety pin, try the garment on the child and adjust the elastic to fit. Trim the ends of the elastic, if necessary. Then overlap the ends of the elastic ½" (13mm), pin them together so the edges are even and stitch across several times to secure (B). Adjust the elastic so that the stitched ends are pulled into the casing. Be careful not to twist the elastic as you do this. Edgestitch the casing opening closed.*

B

To be extra sure that the elastic will not roll or curl when the child is wearing the garment, do the following after the elastic has been inserted into the casing: Adjust the fullness of the garment on the elastic so that it's evenly divided between front and back. Secure the elastic to the garment at each intersecting seam with a pin. Working on the right side of the garment and holding the casing area flat, stitch through the elastic and the casing along the groove formed by the seamline.

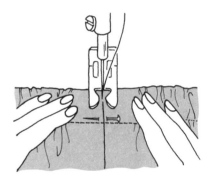

For more information:

see CASINGS.

on Overcasting and Zigzag Stitching, see under MACHINE STITCHING.

see OVERLOCK STITCHING.

on Marking Placement Lines, see under WHAT TO KNOW BEFORE YOU SEW.

Embroidery

Add a row of ducks marching across a playsuit. Monogram a special shirt. Create a border design that echoes the colors and patterns of the fashion fabric. Cover up a worn spot on an old garment or do something fun with a new one. The art of hand or machine embroidery lets you do all this and more.

Machine embroidery is a fast, easy way to decorate or personalize large areas quickly. Hand embroidery is a custom touch that's a labor of love. Although it is more time-consuming than machine embroidery, it has the advantage of being a "take-along" project—you can do it while watching television, waiting for an appointment, even riding on a bus, train or airplane.

If you're a beginner, the easiest fabrics to embroider are light-to medium-weight wovens such as linen, muslin, gingham and broadcloth. However, almost any fabric can be embroidered. Even knits, once considered too stretchy for successful embroidery, can be stabilized for stitching by basting a non-woven, tear-away backing material such as Stitch-n-Tear or Trace Erase to the area which will be embroidered. Once the embroidery is completed, the backing material tears away, leaving no residue.

Use fabrics that have been preshrunk (by you or by the manufacturer), or those that will not shrink more than 1 percent. Otherwise, the fabric shrinks but not your stitches, leaving you with a puckered, unattractive embroidery project.

TRANSFERRING THE DESIGN

Some children's clothing patterns include heat-sensitive transfers for embroidered designs. In addition, there are special patterns that include a variety of embroidery motifs. Both types of patterns include instructions on how to transfer the design to your fabric with the heat of your iron.

You may, however, want to design your own motif. If so, you can transfer it to the fabric using any of the following methods. Although there is no rule that says you can't decide to add embroidery once a garment is completed, you'll find it easier to transfer the embroidery motif to the garment section(s) before they are sewn.

The Tracing Paper Method Use water soluble tracing paper and a ballpoint pen or tracing wheel to transfer the design to the fabric. If your fabric is not washable, be particularly careful not to rest your hand on the coated side of the tracing paper as you work. Otherwise, you may transfer some smudge marks along with your design.

1. *Working on a flat surface, place the tracing paper, wax side down, over the right side of the fabric. Place the design, right side up, on top of the tracing paper.*

2. *Use masking tape or push-pins to hold the layers securely together as you trace over the design with a ballpoint pen or tracing wheel.*

The Pricking Method For this method, you'll use your sewing machine to make a series of holes to transfer the design. You'll also need a special powder, called pounce (available from needlework shops), to rub over the holes and onto the fabric.

1. *Trace the embroidery design onto a crisp paper, such as typing paper.*

2. *Then remove both the top and bobbin threads on your sewing machine and set the stitch length to approximately 8 stitches per inch (per 2.5cm). Stitch slowly and carefully along the design lines, pricking the pattern (A) to create a stencil.*

3. *Put the stencil, right side up, in position on the right side of the fabric and tape in place. Saturate a small felt pad with the pounce and gently rub over the stencil (B). Lift one corner occasionally to make sure enough pounce has gone through.*

4. *Lift off the stencil, taking care not to smudge the pounce. Blow off any excess powder; then, using a sharp dressmaker's pencil or a water soluble marking pen, connect the powder dots to create the design (C).*

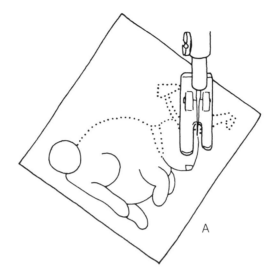

A

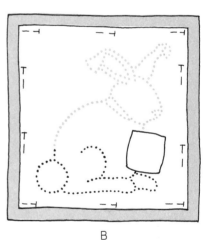

B

C

83

The Transfer Pencil Special hot-iron transfer pencils are available that let you create your own heat transfer designs.

1. *Trace the embroidery design onto heavy tracing paper.*

2. *With a sharp transfer pencil, trace around the embroidery design on the wrong side of the paper.*

3. *Place the embroidery design, wrong side down, on the right side of the fabric. Following the transfer pencil manufacturer's directions, use the heat of your iron to transfer the motif to the fabric.*

HAND EMBROIDERY

Hand embroidery gives you the opportunity to create a limitless array of designs. To make your designs, you'll need to take some time to familiarize yourself with the special needles, threads and techniques used for this exciting craft.

The right size needle is one with an eye large enough for the thread but small enough to avoid leaving a large hole in your fabric. There are three basic types of needles designed for embroidery.

Crewel Long and sharp, with a long, thin eye, these needles are suitable for most types of embroidery threads.

Chenille These needles have a sharp point, a wider eye and are thicker and longer than crewel needles. Use them to embroider with heavier threads and yarns on almost any fabric.

Tapestry Their blunt point and long, rounded eye make these needles suitable for thicker threads and yarns on coarse fabrics.

Unless you have designed your own motif, your project instructions will specify what kind and how many strands of embroidery thread, or floss, to use. Let the weight of the fabric, the desired effect and the compatibility of the thread with your fabric influence your choice of thread.

Six-Strand Embroidery Floss This is a loosely twisted thread that can be separated for embroidering with one, two, three or more strands at a time. Embroidery floss is available in cotton or rayon. It is suitable for many types of embroidery on almost any fabric.

Perle Cotton A twisted two-ply thread, this cotton is available in three thicknesses—3 (the heaviest), 5 and 8. It has a very shiny surface, is suitable for all types of embroidery and can be used on lightweight to heavyweight fabrics.

Crewel Yarn This is a three-strand wool yarn that creates a thicker, more raised effect than either embroidery floss or perle cotton. It works best on mediumweight to heavyweight fabrics. When worked with this yarn, the embroidery is referred to as crewel work.

Narrow Satin Ribbon You can substitute ⅛" (3mm)- or ¹⁄₁₆" (2mm)-wide satin ribbon for embroidery thread on medium- to heavy-weight fabrics. Because the ribbon is wider than thread, your stitches can be longer and your work will go faster. Be sure to keep the ribbon from twisting as you stitch.

Using a Hoop For smooth and pucker-free results, use an embroidery hoop. For hand embroidery, use a 4″, 5″ or 6″ (10cm, 12.5cm or 15cm) hoop. With these smaller sizes, your thumb can reach the center of the hoop, giving you better control of your stitches. Hoops are available in wood and plastic, with an adjustment screw on the outer ring, and in metal with spring tension.

To position your fabric in the hoop, place the inner ring of the hoop on a flat surface. If the hoop has a lip extension, it should be facing up. Place the fabric, right side up, over the ring. Open the adjustment nut on the outer ring, slip it over the fabric and inner ring and tighten the nut. Working around the hoop, pull the fabric taut, keeping the grainline straight, and pushing down on the outer ring to keep it in place.

Once you've mastered a few basic stitches, hand embroidery provides you with the freedom to create just about any type of design you wish.

Blanket Stitch Most often used as a functional, decorative stitch on an edge, this stitch can also be used to outline appliqués or patches.

Work blanket stitch from left to right along the edge of the fabric. Space the stitches evenly, from 3⁄16″ (5mm) to 1⁄4″ (6mm) apart. Secure the thread at the edge, then insert the needle from the right side to the wrong side, anywhere from 3⁄16″ (5mm) to 1⁄2″ (13mm) above the edge. Keeping the thread behind the point of the needle, draw the needle through the loop that is formed and pull the thread taut (A).

To thread the needle with floss, wrap the floss over the needle end securely, as shown, and pinch it to create a crease in the floss (A). Hold the floss, slip the needle from between the floss, push the crease through the eye of the needle (B), then pull the rest of the floss through.

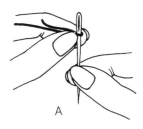

A

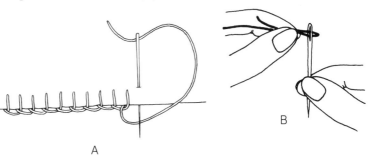

A

B

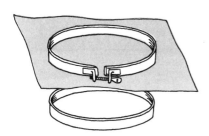

Chain Stitch A favorite stitch for outlining a design or creating a border decoration, this stitch can also be used to fill in areas of a design.

Working on the design line, bring the needle up from the wrong side and make a small loop in front of the needle with the thread. Holding the loop in place with your thumb, insert the needle into the fabric where you first brought it up. Then bring the needle back out at the beginning of the next stitch so that the top of the loop is anchored in place as the needle emerges (B).

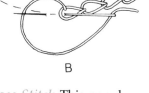

B

Cross Stitch This popular, easy-to-do stitch is used to outline, create borders or fill in areas of design. Because the stitch formation should be uniform, even weave fabrics, such as gingham, are excellent choices for working this stitch.

Work in rows, going across the row from right to left for one half of the cross and then returning back across from left to right to complete it. Bring the needle up from the wrong side at the lower right-hand corner of the first stitch (C). Insert the needle into the upper left-hand corner (D). Then, keeping the needle vertical, come out at the lower right corner of the next stitch (E), creating a diagonal stitch. Continue in this manner all across

the row. Then, to complete the crosses, bring the needle up from the lower left-hand corner of the last stitch and insert it back into the fabric at the upper left-hand corner of the next stitch (F). Bring the needle out at the lower left corner of the next stitch (G). Continue to work from left to right back across the row.

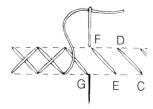

French Knot Use this stitch for filling in a design area, such as the center of a flower, or to create facial features. Since this is a nubby, raised stitch, take care not to flatten it if you're using an embroidery hoop.

Bring the needle up from the wrong side of the fabric. Holding the thread taut in your left hand, wind it twice around the needle while you hold the needle almost flat against the fabric. Insert the needle back into the fabric a thread or two away from where you first brought it up and gently pull the needle and thread through to form the knot (H).

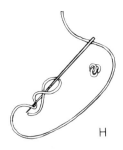

H

For more information:

on Ribbon Embroidery, see under RIBBONS.

Satin Stitch This is most often used as a filler stitch, closely covering areas of the design so that the fabric doesn't show through. To create a smooth surface, keep the stitches at an even tension, flat and close together, and their edges evenly aligned.

Beginning at one end of the shape, bring the needle up from the wrong side at the edge of the area to be filled in. Insert it back into the fabric on the opposite edge. Continue until the design area is covered (I).

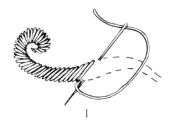

Stem Stitch Generally used to outline, this stitch is also used to create the stems on floral motifs.

Working from left to right, first bring the needle up from the wrong side. Insert it back into the fabric along the design line a short distance from where the needle first emerged. Bring it back out at the end of the previous stitch (J).

For curved lines, keep the thread below the needle as you stitch. For straight lines, keep the thread above the needle.

J

Straight Stitch Used to cover straight design lines or to make an open filling, this stitch can be any length and worked in any direction.

Bring the needle up from the wrong side at one end of the design line and back down at the other, positioning the needle so it comes up close to the end of the next stitch (K).

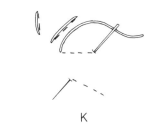

K

MACHINE EMBROIDERY

Machine embroidery, using built-in stitches or the free-motion technique, can be done on almost any type of fabric. If the fabric is lightweight or stretchy, you will need to use a backing material, such as organza, a lightweight fusible interfacing or a nonwoven, tear-away stabilizer specially designed for machine embroidery, such as Stitch-n-Tear or Trace Erase.

You can use regular sewing thread for machine embroidery. However, if your stitches start to bunch up, use the lighter-weight thread specially designed for machine embroidery. Metallics, perle cotton and silk buttonhole twist can be used to create shiny effects. Try hand-winding one of these heavier threads onto the bobbin, being careful not to stretch the thread. Some machines have an adjustment that allows you to loosen

If your machine has a specially designed satin stitch foot or embroidery foot, use it to prevent the stitches from bunching up and to keep the embroidery stitches from being flattened as the presser foot moves over them.

the bobbin tension. If yours does, experiment with adjusting both the upper and lower tensions to produce interesting textural effects. For instance, a couched appearance is achieved by tightening the upper tension, using hand-wound perle cotton on the bobbin, and stitching on the *wrong* side of the fabric.

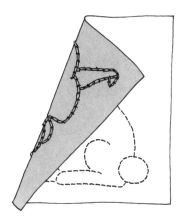

If your machine has a darning foot and throat plate, use them for embroidery, too.

When embroidering a design along the edge of a garment, or on a garment section too small to fit inside an embroidery hoop, enlarge the work surface by basting the fabric to a piece of nonwoven, tear-away stabilizer, such as Stitch-n-Tear or Trace Erase.

Built-in Stitches Many of the sewing machines available today have an assortment of built-in decorative stitches. In general, the more expensive the machine, the greater the variety of stitches. Depending on the machine, you must insert a cam, add a gear, push a button or turn a dial to produce a series of connected motifs.

Your sewing machine manual tells you how to maximize your machine's decorative capabilities. Don't make the mistake of letting all those wonderful stitches and features go to waste. Because children's clothes are usually simple designs, they are a natural place to use the creative capabilities of your sewing machine.

Free-Motion Embroidery Any sewing machine that can make a straight or zigzag stitch can be used to create this type of embroidery. You'll need to insert the fabric into an embroidery hoop, so you can control the placement of the stitches by moving the hoop in the desired direction. You can create an outline stitch or a machine-made satin stitch that imitates the hand-worked satin stitch.

1. *Get the machine ready for free-motion embroidery by doing the following:*

▶ *Remove the presser foot. If it has a separate shank, remove that also.*

▶ *If possible, disengage the feed dogs by covering or lowering them. Your sewing machine manual instructions tell you how to do this.*

▶ *Make sure you have the correct size needle for the thread you're using.*

▶ *Set the stitch length to 0 or the smallest stitch.*

▶ *Loosen the top tension slightly.*

2. *Position the fabric in the embroidery hoop by placing the outer ring on a flat surface, then placing the fabric, right side up,*

For more information:
on Zigzag Stitching, see under
MACHINE STITCHING.

over the ring. Then insert the inner, smaller, ring and tighten the adjustment nut (A). The hoop should be no larger than 8" (20.5cm); otherwise you will not be able to move it freely to both the left and right of the needle.

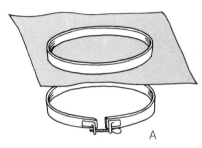

A

3. *Insert the hoop under the needle, then lower the presser bar to engage the upper tension. Holding the upper thread taut, bring the bobbin thread to the surface (B). Then, holding both threads taut and to the left of the needle, take a few small stitches to secure the threads. Clip the end of the thread close to the fabric (C).*

4. *Use the thumb and pinky of each hand to anchor the hoop. Place your middle three fingers on the fabric within the hoop, pressing the fabric firmly near the needle. With your machine running at an even, moderate speed, move the hoop in the desired direction with a slow, gentle, steady motion. To do outline embroidery, direct the hoop with a steady, forward motion (D). To fill in a space with satin stitches, guide the hoop with a steady, back-and-forth motion. If you are filling in a large space with satin stitches, do it in small sections, overlapping the stitches to blend the sections (E).*

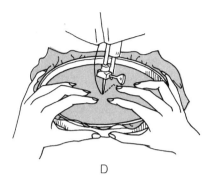

D

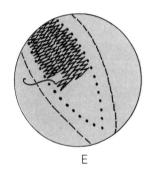

E

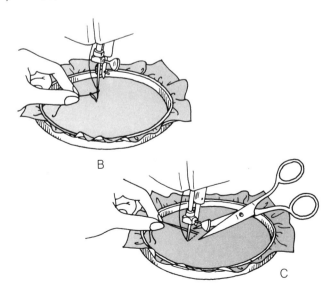

B

C

When adding a machine-embroidered motif such as a monogram or other motif to a napped fabric, such as terry or velour, it is sometimes difficult to achieve clear, straight edges. To solve this problem, begin by tracing the design onto tissue paper. Put a layer of nonwoven stabilizer underneath the area to be embroidered, then place the tissue paper on top of the fabric. Pin baste the layers together. Using the free-motion techniques, outline the design with a straight stitch, then tear away the tissue paper. Stitch over the straight stitches with satin stitches; then tear away the stabilizing material.

Fabrics

Many fabrics that require special handling techniques are extremely popular for children's wear. Stripes and plaids, especially in bright colors, are cheerful and visually stimulating additions to kids' wardrobes. Other fabrics, such as quilteds, corduroys, velvets, velveteens and fake furs, have a textural surface that is very appealing to children.

FAKE FURS

Fake furs are available in a range of fabrications, from the frankly fake to those that imitate the real thing. For best results, select a pattern that is specifically recommended for fake furs.

Layout, Cutting and Marking
▶ *Always follow the "With Nap" layout and always cut out the pattern pieces one layer at a time.*

▶ *Use long, fine, straight pins to pin the pattern pieces to the wrong side of the fur. On long-haired fakes, give the backing a slight lift as you insert each pin.*

▶ *If the fake fur is very bulky, use masking tape instead of pins to secure the pattern tissue and hold the pattern in place with your hand as you cut.*

▶ *Cut medium- to short-length-pile fake fur with regular shears, giving the fabric a slight lift as you go. Place long-haired types on a padded surface and cut with the point of a razor blade or an X-acto® knife.*

▶ *Mark fake fur on the wrong side with a soft lead pencil or a marking pen.*

Interfacing Use a woven, sew-in interfacing in a weight that is compatible with the fake fur.

Preventing Slippage The pile on the fake fur may cause the top layer to shift as you sew. To adjust for this, do the following, making several sample seams, each at least 12" (30.5cm) long:

▶ *Use a #14 or #16 machine needle and 8 to 10 stitches per inch (per 2.5cm).*

▶ *Hold the fabric taut in front of and behind the presser foot as you sew.*

▶ *Reduce the pressure on the presser foot as much as necessary to prevent shifting.*

▶ *To prevent shifting at intersecting seams, take a small hand stitch on the seam allowance at the point where the seams intersect. Tie off the thread ends, then sew the seam.*

Stitching Tips Although straight seams work best on fake furs, you'll probably have to sew curved ones, too, using the techniques found in the Seams section, pages 154–59, and the methods that follow:

▶ *Use paper clips to hold the seam allowance together as you stitch.*

▶ *After stitching the seam, turn the garment to the right side and use a strong needle to gently pull out any hairs caught in the stitching.*

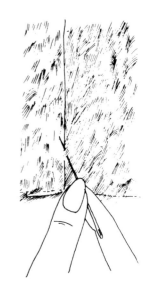

▶ *To reduce bulk, use a small, sharp pair of scissors to trim the pile from the seam allowances as close as possible to the backing fabric.*

Pressing Short-haired fakes can be pressed very lightly on the wrong side with an iron, using a needleboard. Long-haired fakes should be finger pressed, never ironed. To be on the safe side, test press a small scrap to be sure the iron temperature is not too hot and the fabric will withstand pressing without the iron sticking to the backing. If necessary, you can glue the seam allowances in place with rubber cement or fabric glue.

If a seam or hem allowance cannot be pressed or glued flat, use a long running stitch to sew it to the backing fabric.

PLAIDS AND STRIPES

A well-made plaid or striped garment is easy to spot: the bars of color match to form a smooth, unbroken line. The keys to achieving this are careful planning in the layout and cutting stages and careful matching of seams.

Choosing the Pattern Some patterns, such as those with curved or bias seaming, will never look right in a plaid or a stripe. No matter how hard you try, you won't be able to get the bars of color to match. Don't try to second-guess which patterns will work—read the "Fabric Suggestions" provided on the back of the pattern envelope. When a pattern is not suitable for plaids or stripes, it says so.

Choosing the Fabric You will need to purchase more fabric to replace the amount that is "lost" when you lay out the pattern pieces to match the bars of color. As a general rule of thumb for estimating additional yardage, measure the distance between each complete repeat in the pattern, then multiply this amount by the number of main pattern pieces.

Layout Before laying out the pattern, analyze your plaid or stripe to see if it is even or uneven. For a plaid, fold the fabric diagonally through the center of any repeat. If the spaces and colors match, test further by folding the plaid vertically or horizontally through the center of any repeat. For a stripe, fold one of the dominant stripes in half along its length. Then diagonally fold back a corner of the fabric. If all the color bars match, the plaid or stripe is an even design (A, B); if they do not, it's an uneven design (C, D). To make your sewing life simpler, try to choose an even plaid or stripe whenever possible.

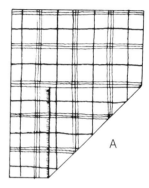

A

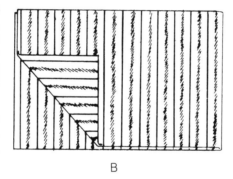

B

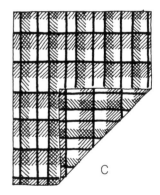

C

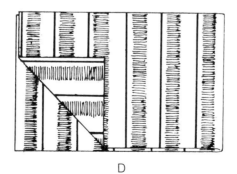

D

Regardless of whether the design is even or uneven, follow the "With Nap" layout. To insure a perfect match, lay out the pieces on a single layer of fabric. If two sections are required, such as a left front and right front or two sleeves, pin and cut the first one, then flip the pattern piece over and cut out the second one.

▶ Begin with the main front pattern piece, placing it so that the most obvious crosswise bar of color falls at the hemline and the most obvious lengthwise bar falls at the center front.

▶ As you lay out the remaining pattern pieces, match the bars of color to the first pattern piece along the seamlines, *not the cutting lines.*

▶ When you get to the sleeve, you will probably find that you cannot match it exactly to both the front and back bodice pieces at the armhole seam. In that case, match it at the front.

Small details, such as collars, cuffs, pockets and yokes should also match.

▶ Pin the main pattern pieces in place on the fabric, then locate the areas where the smaller details will join.

▶ Trace the design of the fabric onto the pattern and indicate the colors (E).

▶ Place the pattern piece for the detail section so that it joins or overlaps the main pattern section as it would on the finished garment and trace the design onto the second piece (F).

▶ Position the pattern piece for the detail section on the fabric so that the traced design matches the fabric design and pin it in place.

Preventing Slippage Once you've cut out the pattern pieces so that they will match, you want to make sure they stay matched as you sew. To prevent shifting and slippage during seaming, do one or more of the following:

▶ Pin at frequent intervals, about every 1" to 2" (2.5 to 5cm). Remove the pins as you sew.

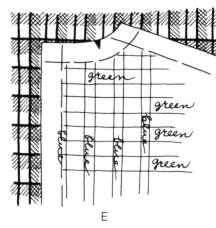

E

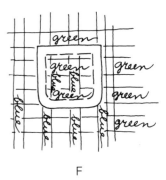

F

When working with plaids, you can eliminate the need to match detail areas, such as collars, cuffs and pockets, by cutting them out on the bias. To establish the bias grainline:

■ Fold the pattern piece in half crosswise close to the center of the grainline arrow (A).

■ Bring the folded edge up to the arrow and crease the pattern along the fold formed (B).

■ Open out the pattern and draw the new grainline along one diagonal crease (C).

A

B

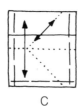

C

▶ *Working on a flat surface, hand baste along the seamlines before stitching.*

▶ *Use double-faced basting tape placed on the seam allowance, slightly away from the seamline. Remove it before pressing the seams.*

▶ *If the seams will not be pressed open, use glue stick.*

QUILTED FABRICS

Quilted fabrics are made of two layers of fabric with a filler, usually a polyester batting, sandwiched in between. Single-faced quilted fabrics have a layer of fashion fabric on one side and a layer of tricot on the other. Double-faced quilteds have fashion fabric on both sides and are reversible.

Most of the special techniques for working with quilteds are for reducing bulk and preventing the batting from being flattened.

Choosing a Pattern Select a pattern with a minimum of design details. Avoid styles that have gathers, tucks, pleats or many seams. If this is your first experience working with quilteds, look for a pattern that specifically recommends them in the "Fabric Suggestions."

Layout and Cutting

▶ *When planning your layout, make sure all the lines of quilting stitches run in the same di-*

rection on all the main pattern pieces.

▶ *Because quilted fabric is usually quite thick, cut your pattern pieces one layer at a time.*

▶ *Use tailor's chalk, pins or a marking pen to mark matching points and symbols. Because of the thickness of the fabric, a tracing wheel will not be accurate.*

▶ *If possible, reduce bulk by using a coordinated, unquilted, fabric for side seam pockets, under collars and facings.*

Interfacing Always use a sew-in interfacing. The steam and pressure required to get a fusible interfacing to adhere to the fabric would flatten the quilt batting.

Stitching Tips

▶ *Staystitch all the edges of all the garment sections. This secures the quilting stitches and helps flatten the edges, making them easier to handle.*

▶ *If the quilting stitches are far apart, trim the batting from the seam allowances and darts wherever possible.*

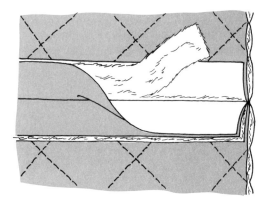

▶ *Use topstitched seams wherever possible to hold the seam allowances securely in place.*

▶ *To prevent shifting of layers as you stitch, pin at frequent intervals, hand baste or use glue stick or double-faced basting tape.*

▶ *Bias bindings make a great edge finish, particularly on double-faced quilted fabric. If the pattern does not already call for binding as an edge finish, trim the entire seam allowance away on the edge to be bound.*

Pressing Set the iron to the correct setting for the side of the fabric being pressed and press lightly to avoid flattening the batting.

VELVETS, VELVETEENS AND CORDUROYS

Velvet is one of the most fragile fabrics used in children's wear, corduroy is one of the most durable ones and velveteen lies somewhere in the middle. However, all three types have a short, dense pile which creates many similarities in the way they are handled.

Layout, Cutting and Marking The number one rule is to lay out all the pattern pieces according to the "With Nap" layout. If you don't use this kind of layout, some parts of the garment will appear to be a slightly different color because of the way the light hits the pile.

Because velvet mars easily, always keep the pins within the seam allowance and remove them as soon as possible after cutting out the garment. Velvet also has a tendency to slip, so cut it out one layer at a time and don't let any excess hang over the edge of your cutting surface.

Use tailor's chalk or a marking pen to mark on the wrong side of these fabrics.

Interfacing Fusible interfacing can be used on corduroy and on velveteen. Contrary to popular belief, it can also be used on some velvets. The key is the fiber content: the velvet must be made of 100 per cent cotton or have a cotton pile and a rayon backing. On other velvets, with rayon and acetate or rayon and silk fiber contents, use a sew-in interfacing.

Stitching Tips The layers of pile fabrics have a tendency to slide and shift as you stitch. To prevent this:

▶ *Pin layers carefully and at close intervals within the seam allowance or hand baste the seams.*

▶ *Make sure your machine tension is loosely balanced.*

▶ *Reduce the tension on the presser foot.*

▶ *As you stitch the seam, stop at regular intervals and, with the needle still in the fabric, raise the presser foot. This allows the fabric to relax.*

Pressing Napped fabrics should always be pressed from the wrong side. Place a needle-board, a thick terry cloth towel or a scrap of the fabric face up on the ironing board.

When pressing velvet, use only the steam from the iron and the tips of your fingers. *Never* rest the iron on the velvet; it will crush and mat the pile.

For more information:

on Hand Basting and Running Stitches, see under HAND SEWING.

see INTERFACING.

see MACHINE STITCHING.

on Topstitched Seams, see under SEAMS.

on Marking and Pressing, see under WHAT TO KNOW BEFORE YOU SEW.

Facings

Facings at garment edges, such as necklines and armholes, provide a finish that both conceals and protects the raw edges. Facings are usually made from the same fabric as the garment. However, if the outer fabric is bulky, such as fake fur, you might wish to use a lighter-weight fabric; or you can make contrast facings for a purely decorative effect.

Before the facing is attached, stabilize the garment edge with interfacing. Your pattern instructions tell you where and how to apply the interfacing.

Two of the most common fabric facings are the shaped facing and the extended facing.

SHAPED

This type of facing is cut to the shape of the garment area it finishes.

1. *If the complete facing contains more than one section, begin by stitching these sections together along the appropriate seamlines as indicated on your pattern instructions (A). Match the pattern markings carefully so*

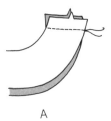

A

that the completed facing forms a perfect curve (B) or straight line. Trim the seam allowance diagonally at the notched edge.

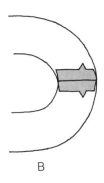

B

2. *Finish the outer edge of the facing according to the method most suitable for your garment and fabric. With right sides together, pin the facing to the garment and stitch.*

3. *To eliminate bulk, trim and grade the seam allowances, cutting the facing narrower than the garment seam allowance. Trim any corners diagonally, and clip or notch just to, but not through, the stitching in any curved areas (C). Press the facing edge flat along the seamline, first on one side, then on the other.*

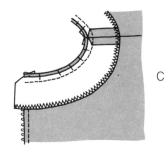

C

4. *If the facing edge is not eventually going to be edgestitched or topstitched in place, understitch close to the seamline through all seam allowances.*

5. *Turn the facing to the wrong side of the garment and press it. As you press, roll the seam slightly toward the facing side (D). This is called* **favoring,** *and it helps keep the facing from showing on the outside of your garment.*

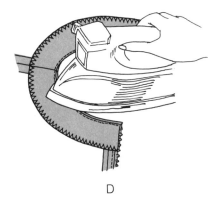

D

6. *Even if you understitch, top-stitch or edgestitch the facing, it's a good idea to secure it at the seams. Either tack it in place by hand (E) or fuse a small piece of fusible web between the facing and the garment seam allowances (F).*

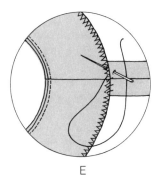

E

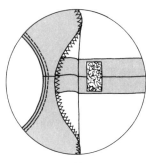

F

EXTENDED

This type of facing is simply an extension of the garment. It is cut in one piece with the garment, and then folded to the inside. Use it to finish edges cut on a straight grain which can be extended to make a fold at the edge of the garment, instead of a separate facing attached with a seam.

1. *If the complete facing contains more than one section, begin by stitching these sections together along the appropriate seamlines, as indicated in your pattern instructions (A).*

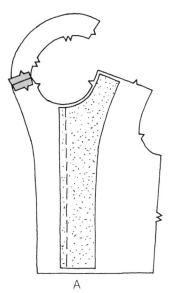

A

2. *Finish the outer edge of the facing according to the method most suitable for your garment and fabric.*

3. *Turn the facing to the right side along the foldline, matching notches and/or symbols, and pin in place. Stitch the seam. To eliminate bulk, trim and grade the seam allowances, cutting the facing narrower than the garment seam allowance. Trim any corners diagonally, and clip or notch just to, but not through, the stitching in any curved areas (B).*

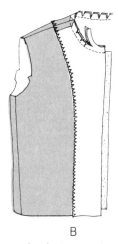

B

4. *Turn the facing to the inside and press it flat.*

5. *Refer to steps 4 to 6 of the Shaped Facing, page 96, for understitching, pressing and securing the facing.*

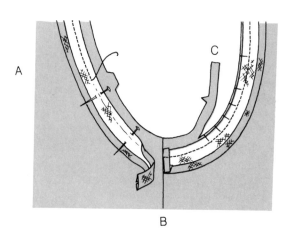

A

C

B

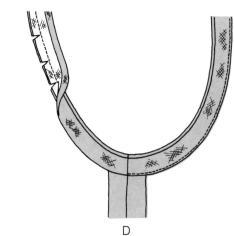

D

BIAS TAPE

Double-fold bias tape makes a quick and easy facing that can be shaped to match any curved or straight garment edge. It is available in several widths and a variety of colors.

1. *Cut the bias tape as long as the area to be faced, plus ½" (13mm) for turning under the raw ends. Unfold the tape and press out the center crease. Open out one long edge of the bias tape. With right sides together, pin the tape to the garment edge, matching the creaseline of the tape to the seamline of the garment (A). Be careful not to stretch the tape. Fold the short ends ¼" (6mm) to the wrong side so that they will meet when the tape is turned to the inside of the garment (B).*

2. *Stitch along the creaseline of the tape. Trim the garment seam allowance even with the edge of the tape; then clip the curve just to the stitching line, through all thicknesses (C).*

3. *Fold the bias tape to the wrong side of the garment, favoring the seam slightly to the inside. Press, then machine stitch or slipstitch the tape in place along the entire edge (D).*

If you are using the Flat Construction Method and substituting bias tape for a fabric facing, apply the tape first; then stitch the underarm and/or side seams, stitching through the tape. Then turn the bias tape to the inside of the garment and complete as described previously in step 3.

For more information:

see FUSIBLE WEB.

on Slipstitching and Tacking, see under HAND SEWING.

on Edgestitching, Topstitching and Understitching, see under MACHINE STITCHING.

on Clipping, Grading, Notching and Trimming, see under SEAMS.

Flat Construction Method

Your sewing will go faster if you organize it according to the Flat Construction Method. The procedure is to complete as many small details as possible on each section of the garment while it is still flat, leaving the major seams, such as side seams and underarm seams, open. It is often easier to do machine stitching of details on a small, flat section than an entire garment, especially on small children's garments.

Some of the easy-to-sew patterns are assembled according to this method. However, you can readily adapt the method to any pattern by reorganizing your sewing procedures into the following steps:

1. *Complete small detail areas, such as darts, pockets, zippers, shoulder straps and ties, and attach to the main garment pieces (A).*

2. *Stitch garment sections together along any horizontal seamlines, such as shoulder seams, yoke seams or waistline seams (B).*

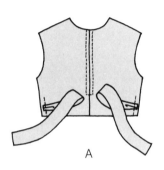

A

B

99

3. *Attach major detail areas, such as collars and facings. Finish and attach cuffs to sleeves. Finish sleeves up to the underarm seam and attach to the garment at the armhole. Apply buttonholes (C).*

4. *Stitch the garment together at underarms and sides in one continuous seam (D).*

5. *Complete all the finishing details, such as hems, snaps and buttons.*

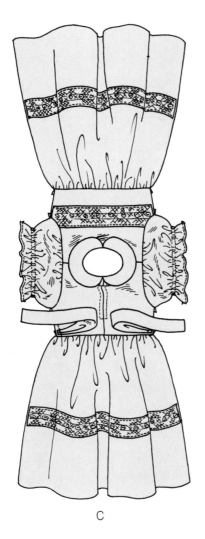

C

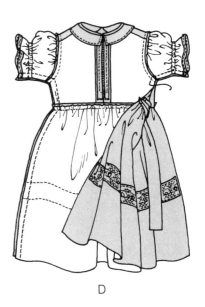

D

Fusible Web

One of today's modern conveniences, fusible web is a bonding agent that is used to join two layers of fabric *without* stitches. Before fusing, it looks like non-woven netting; when properly fused, the fibers dissolve to adhere the fabric together. Sold in narrow strips or by the yard (meter), as a sewing aid, fusible web has many uses, including hemming, applying trims and appliqués, mending and tacking down the edges of facings. Fusible web can also be used in place of temporary basting stitches for positioning pockets or appliqués (A) or to hold layers in position for making fabric belts and belt carriers (B).

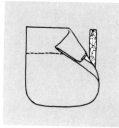

A

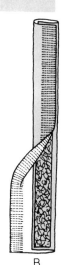

B

Fusible web is strictly a bonding agent. Don't confuse it with fusible interfacing which adds an extra layer of fabric that reinforces, stabilizes and/or adds shape to an area of the garment.

There are several brands of fusible web. Although each comes with its own specific product directions, there are some general guidelines to keep in mind.

1. *Complete all preliminary pressing before positioning the web on the garment. Make markings for trims and appliqués clear and precise so the web can be positioned accurately. Complete facings. Measure hems accurately. Trim and press up hem allowances.*

2. *Cut the fusible web to the required shape and size. If your particular sewing technique requires long strips of fusible web, you can use the precut strips or cut your own from a large piece. A quick way to do this is to fold the web several times, mark the width you need and cut once through all thicknesses (C).*

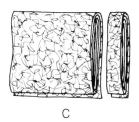

C

It's all too easy to get little pieces of fusible web stuck to your ironing board cover. To prevent this, protect the surface by covering it with an old sheet when you fuse. If fusible web gets onto your iron, clean it with one of the commercial iron cleaners.

3. *Insert the fusible web between the layers of fabric and fuse in place, using a press cloth and the recommended amount of heat, steam and time (D).*

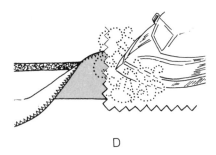

D

4. *Although fusible web is not generally recommended as a hemming technique if you plan to let the hem down, it can be removed by reapplying heat and steam to the bonded area. While the fabric is warm, pull the two layers apart. Continue applying heat and steam to remove as much of the residue as possible. Whatever residue remains can be removed with denatured alcohol. Be sure to test first on a scrap of fabric, as some fabrics are not tolerant of alcohol.*

Fusible web can also be used to invisibly mend a rip in a garment.

1. *With pinking shears, cut out a patch of self-fabric and a piece of fusible web slightly larger than the rip.*

2. *Align the cut edges of the rip so that they are almost invisible.*

3. *Working on the wrong side of the garment, center the fusible web over the rip. Place the patch of self-fabric, right side down, over the web and fuse in place.*

The easy way to cut out fusible web to the exact same size as an appliqué or a fabric patch is to place the fabric on top of the web and cut out both shapes at the same time.

Gathering

For a soft, graceful way to add fullness to a child's garment, gathers can be used sparingly or abundantly, to produce a hint of fullness in a sleeve cap or a dirndl skirt, or rows of flounces adorning a party dress.

Two rows of long stitches, made either by hand or machine, are used to create gathers. The two rows help the fabric to fall into smooth, even folds. In addition, you have a safeguard in case the threads in one of the rows break.

If you are using gathering to create a ruffle, see Ruffles, pages 151–53, for more information.

BY HAND

Although the majority of gathering is done by machine, there may be times when you prefer to do some of your gathering by hand. Very delicate fabrics or narrow trims, particularly those used for garments such as christening dresses, are often easier to gather by hand.

To gather by hand, use a running stitch. See page 109. Hand gathering is easier if you work on each individual fabric piece before the pieces are joined to each other.

BY MACHINE

1. *To reduce bulk, trim any seam allowances that will be crossed by the gathering stitches. Trim the seam allowance diagonally across the intersecting stitching line (A).*

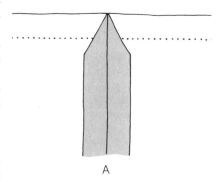

A

2. *Set your machine for a longer stitch length. For lightweight to mediumweight fabrics, try 8 to 10 stitches per inch (3 per cm). Loosen the upper tension slightly to make it easier to pull the bobbin thread later on. Test gather on a scrap of fabric and lengthen the stitch, if necessary. Heavier fabrics will require a longer stitch length, and soft or gauzy fabrics, a shorter length.*

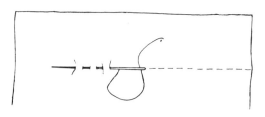

3. *With your fabric right side up, stitch one row on the seamline, leaving long thread ends at either side. Stitch a second row, ¼" (6mm) above the first, on the seam allowance. Keep the stitching lines parallel—they should never cross (B).*

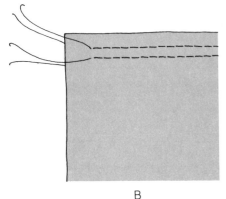

B

If the gathering stitches cross intersecting seams on large garment sections, such as a skirt or a hemline flounce, stop stitching when you reach one side of the seam. Break the thread and resume stitching directly on the other side of the seam. Be sure to leave long thread ends (C).

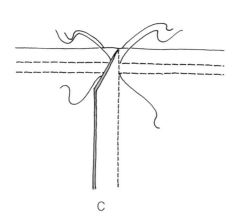

C

JOINING SECTIONS

The gathered section is usually joined to another section that is not gathered, such as a skirt to a waistband or a ruffle to the edge of a yoke.

1. *Working with right sides together, and with the section to be gathered facing you, pin the two sections together, matching the raw edges and the construction markings. To keep the bobbin threads from pulling out as you gather, put a pin at one end of each section of gathering stitches and then wind the thread ends around the pin in a figure eight. Gently pull the bobbin threads from the other end, using one hand to slide the fabric along the threads. Use your other hand to adjust the gathers, keeping them evenly distributed (A).*

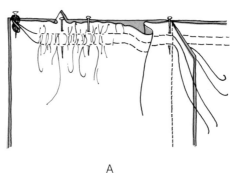

A

To make super-quick gathers, place a piece of crochet cotton or buttonhole twist just above the seamline and zigzag over it. Position the needle so that, on the left swing, it goes into the fabric exactly at the seamline. To gather, push the fabric along the cord. Use a zipper foot to stitch the gathered section to the ungathered one, stitching just below the cord. Then pull out the cord.

2. *Pin baste the gathered section to the ungathered section, making sure that all construction markings match. Working with the gathered side up so that you can keep it smooth and even as you sew, stitch the two sections together along the seamline. Since you are able to see the gathers as you sew, you will also be able to prevent any unwanted tucks or pleats from forming (B).*

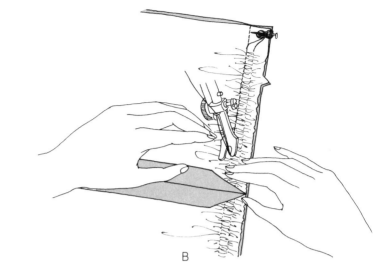

B

STAYING GATHERS

Seam binding can be used as a stay to reinforce or finish off a gathered seam. This may be included as a feature of your pattern, or you may wish to add it, particularly if you are working with a fabric that has a loose weave.

Add the stay after the gathered section is joined to another section. Position the seam binding on the seam allowance, with the lower edge next to the seamline. Stitch along the lower edge, through all the layers. Trim the seam allowances even with the top edge of the stay. If your fabric has a tendency to ravel, machine zigzag or overcast along the top edge of the seam binding, through all layers (C).

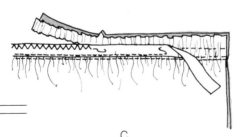

C

If you use a different color thread in the bobbin, you will be able to immediately identify which thread to pull. And if you stitch the row of gathering stitches from the right side, the bobbin thread will be easy to see when you pull up the gathers.

If you are gathering a small area, there's no need to break your threads at the end of each row of gathering stitches. Instead, sew the first row along the seamline, pivot, take two stitches perpendicular to the first row on the seam allowance, pivot and sew the second row of stitches parallel to the first row.

For more information:

on Pivoting, see under APPLIQUÉ.

on Pin Basting, see under BASTING.

on Running Stitch, see under HAND SEWING.

on Overcasting and Zigzag Stitching, see under MACHINE STITCHING.

on Pressing Gathers, see under WHAT TO KNOW BEFORE YOU SEW.

Hand Sewing

Although machine stitching is the fastest way to get things done, there are times when hand sewing is the best way. Also, because hand sewing is portable and can be done while you're waiting for an appointment, watching television or talking on the telephone, it may be more efficient if certain parts of the garment, such as hems and buttons, are done by hand.

CHOOSING THE RIGHT NEEDLE

Your goal is to choose a needle that is fine enough to slip through the fabric easily, but strong enough so it won't bend or break. Generally, the finer the weave or the more sheer the fabric, the sharper and more slender the needle should be.

Hand sewing needles are classified into types and are numbered according to size. The largest needles have the smallest numbers. For general hand sewing, they range from 1, the largest size, to 12, the smallest size. For most of your sewing, the sizes from 5 to 10 will be the best choice.

Types of needles include:

▶ *Sharps—medium-length needles with small, round eyes. These are suitable for almost all weights of fabric.*

▶ *Calyx-eye—similar to sharps, but with a slot, rather than a round eye. These are also called self-threading needles.*

▶ *Ball-points—similar to sharps but with rounded points that allow the needle to penetrate between the yarns on knit fabric without snagging.*

▶ *Betweens—shorter than sharps, with small, round eyes. These are good for detailed handwork and hand quilting.*

▶ *Milliners—longer than sharps and betweens, with small, round eyes. These are useful for sewing long basting stitches easily.*

threads to synthetic fabrics. If in doubt, use cotton-wrapped polyester thread, an all-purpose thread that can be safely used on most fabrics. When sewing on knits, regardless of the fiber content, it's best to use a synthetic thread because it will provide the required stretchability.

The size of mercerized cotton thread is indicated by numbers. The higher the number, the finer the thread, with #50 as the midpoint. Letters are used to indicate the size of silk thread—A is fine and D is heavy. Some companies simply label the thread with words such as "all-purpose," "lightweight," "extra strong," etc.

SECURING THE THREAD

If your hand stitches are temporary ones, such as basting stitches, go ahead and knot the thread. The knot will be removed along with the temporary stitches. However, if your hand stitches are permanent, a tack is more secure.

Working with an unknotted length of thread, take a small stitch in the fabric at the begin-

---

Don't spend valuable time hunting for the right needle. Once your hand sewing task is completed, return the needle to its original, labeled package.

CHOOSING THE RIGHT THREAD

When sewing on woven fabrics, the general rule is to match the type of thread to the type of fabric—natural fiber threads to natural fabrics, synthetic fiber

Can't find the right color thread? Choose one that is a shade darker than your fabric—it will appear slightly lighter when sewn.

ning of the stitching line. While holding the thread end with your fingers to keep the entire length of thread from pulling through, take several stitches directly over the first stitch. When you come to the end of the stitching line, repeat, making another tack. If the thread ends will be visible on your finished garment, clip them off close to the tacks.

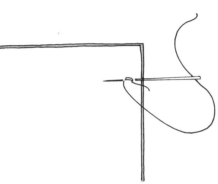

TYPES OF STITCHES

Since there are several hand stitches for different needs and situations, always refer to this section when you're not sure which one to use.

Backstitch Because this stitch is one of the strongest hand stitches, it is particularly useful when mending hard-to-reach seams. Although the stitches overlap on the underside, they imitate a machine straight stitch on the upper side. Stitches on the top side should be all the same length. Stitches on the underside will be twice as long.

Working with the right sides of the fabric together and following the seamline, bring the needle up through the fabric and insert it one stitch [$\frac{1}{16}$" to $\frac{1}{8}$" (2 to 3mm)] back. Bring the needle out again, one stitch ahead on

the seamline. Continue, inserting the needle in the end of the last stitch and bringing it out one stitch ahead.

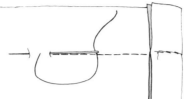

Basting Stitch Hand basting is one of several alternatives for holding garment pieces together temporarily. As a general rule, these stitches should be about 1" (2.5cm) apart and $\frac{1}{2}$" (13mm) long. Make them a little shorter in detail areas that require more control.

Blindstitch Frequently used for hemming and for holding facings in place, this stitch is inconspicuous on both the right and wrong sides of the garment.

Finish the raw edges of the hem or the facing with a technique that is appropriate for your

To make it easier to thread your needle, cut the thread on an angle. Avoid the temptation to bite or break the thread, as those rough ends will be almost impossible to navigate through the eye of a needle.

To keep your thread from knotting or tangling, and for easier control as you sew, keep the length of your thread to not more than 20" (51cm) from knot to needle.

fabric. Roll this finished edge back about $\frac{1}{4}$" (6mm) as you sew. Take a short, horizontal stitch through one thread on the garment side, then pick up a thread from the hem or facing diagonally above and pull the needle through. Repeat this diagonal stitching, going back and forth between the garment and the hem or facing. Do not pull the stitches tight.

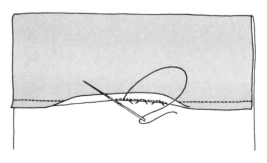

If your thread becomes twisted, let the needle dangle freely. It will automatically begin to turn, untwisting most of the thread. To finish the process, run your thumb and index finger along the length of the thread.

Catchstitch This stitch has the advantage of holding two layers of fabric securely together, while still providing a degree of flexibility. It is most often used to attach the raw edges of facings or sew-in interfacings to the wrong side of the garment, to hand sew pleats or tucks in linings and to secure hems in stretchy fabrics such as knits.

Working from left to right, take a small horizontal stitch in the top layer of fabric a short distance from the edge. Then, working diagonally above the first stitch, take a stitch in the layer underneath, inserting the needle from right to left. This second stitch should be a scant distance above the edge of the top layer. Continue, alternating the stitching along the edge in a zigzag manner. Do not pull the stitches tight.

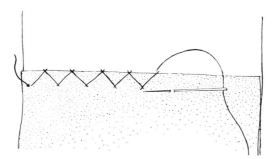

Hemming Stitch As the name implies, this stitch is the most commonly used one for hemming, particularly if the hem edge is finished with seam binding. Take a small, inconspicuous stitch in the garment, and at the same time, bring the needle diagonally up through the edge of the seam binding or hem edge and pull the needle through. Continue in this manner, spacing stitches about ¼" (6mm) apart. Do not pull the stitches tight.

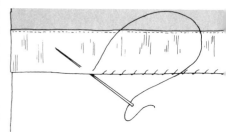

Overcast Stitch This finishing stitch can be used in place of a machine zigzag or overcast stitch to keep raw edges from raveling. It does not matter if you work from the right or the left—choose the direction that is most comfortable for you. Insert the needle about ¹⁄₁₆" to ⅛" (2 to 3mm) from the edge, and make diagonal stitches over the edge, spacing them evenly apart and at a uniform depth. Some people like to take two or three stitches on the needle before pulling up the thread, to make the work go faster.

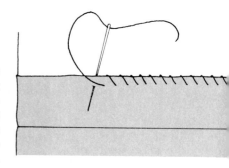

Running Stitch Use this stitch for easing, gathering and tucking, as well as for mending and sewing seams that are not subject to much strain.

Take small forward stitches by evenly weaving the needle in and out of the fabric several times, then pulling the thread through. The number of stitches you can pick up at one time will depend on the length of your needle and the thickness of your fabric. For easing and gathering, the stitches should be $\frac{1}{16}$" to $\frac{1}{4}$" (2 to 6mm) long; for permanent seams, stitches should be $\frac{1}{16}$" to $\frac{1}{8}$" (2 to 3mm) long.

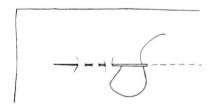

Slipstitch For an almost invisible stitch that is particularly useful for hemming turned-under edges, as well as holding pockets and trims in place, use the slipstitch.

Insert the needle into the folded edge and slide it inside the fold for a short distance. Bring the point of the needle out and take a small stitch in the

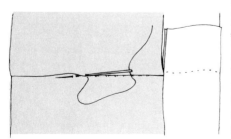

fabric underneath, directly under where the needle emerged. Pull the needle through, insert it back into the fold and repeat, making stitches that are $\frac{1}{8}$" to $\frac{1}{4}$" (3 to 6mm) apart and evenly spaced.

Tack Several small stitches used to inconspicuously secure one part of a garment to another, such as the neck facing to the shoulder seam allowances, are called tacks. Take a small stitch in the layer underneath, then bring the needle diagonally up through the edge of the top layer. Continue in this manner, spacing stitches $\frac{1}{16}$" to $\frac{1}{8}$" (2 to 3mm) apart, then take a few on top of each other when you want to stop.

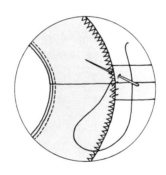

This stitch is used to hold two finished edges together with tiny, straight, even stitches. It is most often used to join lace edging or to attach ribbon to a garment. Insert the needle at a right angle from the underneath edge through to the upper edge, picking up only one or two threads at a time. Stitches should be close together as shown.

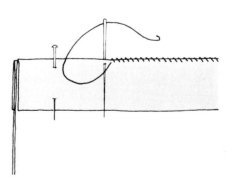

For more information:

on Overcasting and Zigzag Stitching, see under MACHINE STITCHING.

on Finishing Edges, see under SEAM FINISHES.

Hems

Hemlines on adult clothes are subject to the whims of fashion; on children's garments, to the child's age and growth rate. Particularly for young children, safety, not fashion, determines the proper length. Toddlers' pants can be any length. Skirts, however, should be short so they don't get tangled when little legs try to crawl and walk. As girls get older, their skirts can be longer.

MEASURING THE HEM

Since it's not realistic to expect small children to stand still while a hem is being marked, don't even try to measure very small or very active children. Instead, measure a garment that is already the proper length.

It's easiest to determine garment lengths and mark them on the pattern tissue before the garment is cut out. Mark the length on the pattern tissue or garment while it's laid out on a table, measuring from the waistline seam or underarm at the sides. Finished dress, skirt and pants lengths should be included in your record of the child's measurements.

Children's garments often get too short before they get too tight. Consider adjusting your pattern to allow for this growth. See Room to Grow, pages 26–35, for suggestions.

Using a marking method suitable for your fabric, transfer the hemline markings from the pattern tissue to the garment sections.

Once you get to the point where the garment is finished except for the hem, check the garment length. Hand baste or pin baste the hem in place and have the child try the garment on. To avoid scratching the child, use safety pins, not straight pins. If the finished garment has a belt or sash, make sure the child is wearing it or, if you haven't finished it yet, one that is similar. A belt or sash can change the garment length and the way it hangs.

For bias or circular skirts, it is essential to check the garment length. Garments cut on the bias have a tendency to stretch and grow at the hemline. If the fabric stretches, the hemline will need to be adjusted to make it even. Let the garment hang for at least 24 hours before you have the child try it on.

PLAIN HEM

This basic hem has little or no fullness. You can hand sew it in place, using one of the stitches described in the Hand Sewing section, pages 107–9, or stitch it in place by machine as described in the Machine Stitching section, pages 122–27.

When you are satisfied with the garment length, use the hemline marking as a guide to even out the raw edge of the hem allowance. You'll need to do this because, no matter how careful a sewer you are, slight cutting or stitching differences can occur, resulting in an uneven hem. With a ruler or a hem gauge, check the depth of the hem allowance along the entire circumference (A). On a child's garment the hem depth is usually 2½" to 3" (6.5 to 7.5cm). Correct any errors with chalk or a

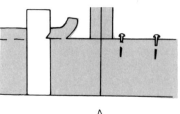

A

marking pen or pencil, then trim.

To reduce bulk in the seam allowance area and to prevent ridges from forming along the seams once the hem is pressed, trim the seam allowances on any seam that crosses the hem. Trim them to ¼" (6mm) from the raw edge of the garment to the hemline (B) only if you have no plans to enlarge the garment at a future date by letting out the side seams.

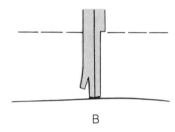

B

Press the hem, following the guidelines on page 42.

Finish the raw edge with the seam finish that is most appropriate for your fabric and your garment. Hand sew or machine stitch the hem in place.

EASED HEM

If the garment has a shaped hem with excess fullness that must be controlled, the hem allowance should be eased. Even out the hem allowance and trim the seam allowances as for the plain hem. Then, using long stitches, from the wrong side stitch ¼" (6mm) from the raw edge. Pull up the bobbin thread every few inches (centimeters) to adjust the ease; then shrink out the fullness as much as possible with a steam iron, inserting strips of brown paper between the hem allowance and the garment.

Finish the raw edge with the best seam finish for your fabric and your garment. Hand sew the hem in place using a stitch suitable for your fabric.

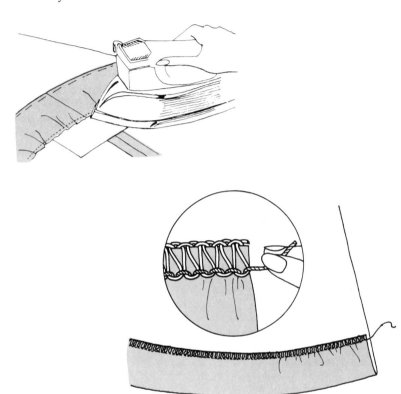

To finish the raw edge *and* ease the hem by machine, use the overlock stitch. Loosen the needle thread tension and overlock the raw edge, then pull up on the needle thread to ease in the fullness. Hand sew or machine topstitch the hem in place.

HAND-SEWN HEM

Because durability is a very important factor in children's clothes, most hems are done by machine. However, there will be times when you will prefer a hand-sewn hem. Following are the four most frequently used hand stitches for hems. See the Hand Sewing section, pages 107–9, for information on how to do each stitch. Your choice of hem finish influences your choice of hem stitches:

▶ *Blindstitch is most frequently used with the stitched-and-pinked seam finish on all fabrics, as well as with the zigzagged finish on heavier fabrics.*

111

▶ *Catchstitch is used with the zigzagged or stitched-and-pinked finish on lightweight to medium-weight fabrics and on all knits that require some stretchability in the hem.*

▶ *Hemming stitch is ideal when the raw edge of the hem allowance is finished with seam binding.*

▶ *Slipstitch is a good stitch to use for any hem that has a folded edge finish.*

MACHINE-STITCHED HEM

Children's clothes are subject to the wear and tear of active play, the stress of repeated launderings and the pulling and tugging that go with learning how to dress. To survive all this activity, a machine-stitched hem is frequently the best choice. The type depends entirely on the fabric you are using.

Narrow This is an easy hem to do. Use it on sheer and lightweight fabrics. Because of the narrow hem allowance, very little easing is required. However, there is no room to let the hem down at a future date. This is an important consideration if you use this as a finish at the lower edge of skirts, pants and sleeves. It is an excellent, nonbulky finish for the lower edge of blouses and shirts.

Turn up the hem along the hemline and press. Trim the hem allowance to ⅜" or ⅝" (10 or 15cm). Open out the hem allowance, fold the raw edge to the inside of the garment until it touches the crease, then press.

Turn the hem allowance up again along the hemline and stitch along the upper fold (A).

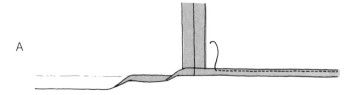

A

If the hem includes a right-angled corner, eliminate bulk in the corner area by using the following mitering procedure:

1. *Turn up and press the hem allowance along the hemline. Open the hem allowance out and fold it up diagonally at the corner. Press along this diagonal foldline to form a crease (B).*

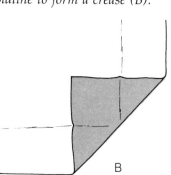

B

2. *Trim off the corner above the crease, leaving ¼" to ⅜" (6 to 10mm) of fabric (C).*

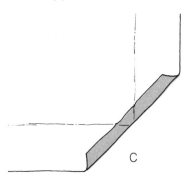

C

3. *Turn the raw edge under so that the edge meets the crease and press. Then fold along the creaseline; the side edges will meet at the corner, covering the cut corner without any bulk (D). Finish the hem according to the pattern instructions or by machine stitching from the wrong side, with the hem facing you. If it is compatible with the detailing on the rest of the garment, add a second row of topstitching along the outside edge of the hem.*

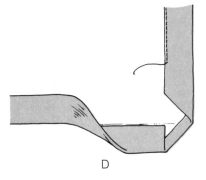

D

Knits For knit fabrics, stitch the hem after the raw edge is turned up once, since knits generally don't ravel and do not require a raw edge finish. Turn up and press the hem allowance, then stitch ¼″ (6mm) from the fold. Trim the hem allowance close to the stitching (A).

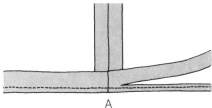

A

Double knits and jersey fabrics can be hemmed by stitching directly along the hemline, using a short, narrow zigzag stitch, and then trimming away the hem allowance as close to the stitching as possible (B). *Avoid stretching the hem as you sew.* Or use the overlock machine, which will stitch and trim the hem at the same time (see Overlock Hem, on the next page). This provides a decorative look that should be compatible with the rest of the garment.

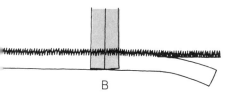

B

Topstitched To make this hem, turn the edge of the garment up along the hemline marking and trim the hem allowance to an even amount. Finish the raw edge with a suitable seam finish. Using either matching or contrasting thread, topstitch the hem parallel to the folded edge. If you are using one row of topstitching, stitch ¼″ (6mm) below the finished edge of the hem allowance: If you are using multiple rows, stitch one row approximately ¼″ (6mm) from the folded edge, then stitch each successive row parallel to the previous row, until the entire hem allowance area is secured (C).

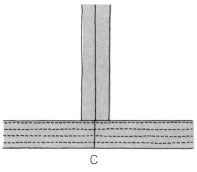

C

Blindstitched If your machine has a built-in blindstitch, you can hem medium-weight fabrics quickly and invisibly. Turn up the fabric along the hemline and press. Finish the raw edge with a method suitable for your fabric. Fold the garment back ¼″ (6mm) below the hem edge. As you stitch the hem, align the stitches so that the straight stitches fall on the hem allowance and the zigzag stitch just catches the folded back edge of the garment (D).

If your machine has a narrow hemmer attachment, use it to fold and stitch the fabric in one step. Guide the fabric by pre-folding it for about 1″ (2.5cm) in front of the foot as you stitch. This attachment works best on lightweight fabrics.

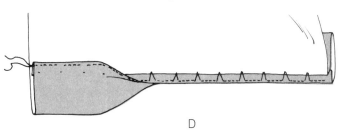

D

113

If you are having difficulty stitching close to the lower edge as you narrow hem, put a strip of nonwoven, tear-away stabilizing material under the stitching line as you sew.

To achieve straight, parallel rows of topstitching, use the toe of your presser foot as a guide. Line up the edge of the garment or the previous row of stitching with the right-hand edge of the right toe of the foot.

OVERLOCK HEM

Take advantage of your overlock machine to create a variety of fast and easy hemming techniques.

Single Overedged This technique can be done on any overlock machine, eliminating double layers of fabric at the hem edge, as well as the time-consuming process of pressing and measuring the hem allowance. Working on the right side of the garment, overlock stitch along the hemline (A).

Narrow or Rolled This hem is suitable for all but loosely woven fabrics. It can be done on some two-thread and most three-thread machines. Consult your machine manual—some machines require a change of foot and/or a different throat plate.

By altering the stitch length and stitch width you can create different effects. Narrow the stitch width to 2mm, then experiment on scraps of your fabric to achieve the desired look. Shorter stitches create a satin edge; longer stitches create a picot or scalloped edge.

In addition to altering the stitch length and width, you'll need to make some tension adjustments to get the edge of the fabric to roll. Loosen the upper looper tension and tighten the lower looper tension. Because the fabric will roll to the underside, overlock the hem from the right side (B).

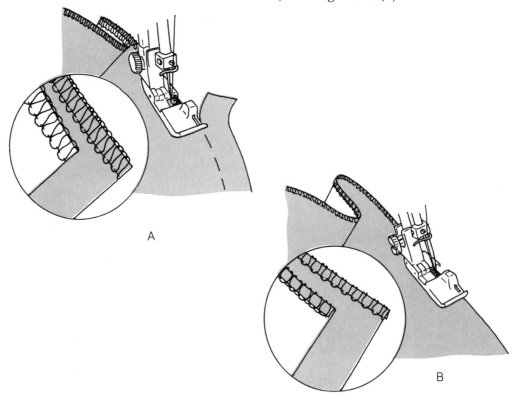

A

B

Ladder This hem, popular on commercial T-shirts and sweatshirts, is easy to do on both two- and three-thread machines. Fold the fabric accordion style, first folding it to the inside along the hemline, then folding the hem allowance and garment back to the outside along the cut edge of the hem allowance. With the fabric right side up and to the left of the cutting knife, overlock stitch along the cut edge of the hem and the second fold, being careful not to cut the folded edge of the garment (A). Pull the fabric open to remove the second fold; the stitches will lie flat, forming a ladder effect on the outside of the garment above the hemline (B).

1. *To insure a smooth appearance on the finished hem, cut the fusible web into long, narrow strips or use precut strips of fusible web.*

2. *Position the web about ¼" (6mm) below the hem edge (C). This will prevent the hem edge from creating a ridge on the right side of the garment and it will keep the web away from the soleplate of your iron. Sometimes it's difficult to keep the strips of web in place as you fuse, particularly if you are working with a shaped hem or a small, narrow area, such as the hem of a child's sleeve or pants leg. In this case, machine baste the web to the hem allowance, ¼" (6mm) below the hem edge, before fusing (D). Then fuse in place.*

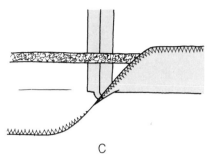

C

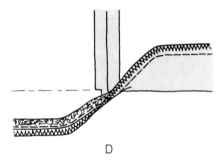

D

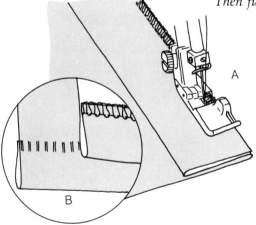

A

B

FUSED HEM

Using fusible web is a fast substitute for machine or hand sewing hems. As with any other hemming technique, it is important to measure, trim and press the hem allowance, then finish the raw edge before securing the hem.

For more information:

see FUSIBLE WEB.

on Topstitching and Zigzag Stitching, see under MACHINE STITCHING.

see OVERLOCK STITCHING.

on Finishing Edges, see under SEAM FINISHES.

on Marking and Pressing, see under WHAT TO KNOW BEFORE YOU SEW.

Hooks and Eyes

Hooks and eyes are two-part closures that are almost always hidden from view when the garment is fastened. There are several types of hooks and eyes and the one you choose depends on the weight of your fabric and the amount of stress that the hook and eye must endure. For example, hooks and eyes used at the waistband of a skirt or a pair of pants must be flatter and sturdier than the ones used at the top of a back neck opening.

The **standard hook and eye** has a brass base with a nickel or a black enamel finish and sizes ranging from fine (0) to heavy (3). Hooks and eyes are packaged with two different types of eyes—curved, for edges that meet, and straight, for lapped edges.

Coat hooks and eyes are designed to be used on outerwear so they are larger than standard hooks and eyes, and the bill of the hook is slightly flattened to

make a snug closure. These hooks and eyes are also available in nickel or black finishes.

Covered hooks and eyes, also larger than the standard hooks and eyes, are particularly good for dressy outerwear made from heavier fabrics. They are available in neutral colors, such as black, brown and beige. Because the thread covering provides a nicer appearance and a less abrasive surface than the all-metal coat hooks and eyes, these closures are often used for fastening fake fur coats and collars.

Waistband hooks and eyes are flat, sturdy closures designed to be used where there is stress and strain, such as the waistband on skirts and pants. They are available in wide and narrow designs, in nickel and black finishes.

Attaching at Edges That Meet

Use the curved eye with the hook. Sew both the hook and the eye to the wrong side of the garment as follows, taking care that the stitches do not show on the outside of the garment:

1. *Position the eye so that the loop extends slightly beyond one edge of the garment. Attach it to the garment by sewing around each hole, and then taking several stitches at each side of the loop (A).*

2. *Position the hook about ¹⁄₁₆"* (2mm) *from the other edge of the garment. Test this position by inserting the hook into the eye. The edges of the garment should meet closely but not overlap. Attach the hook to the garment by sewing around each hole, and then taking several stitches under the bill of the hook (B).*

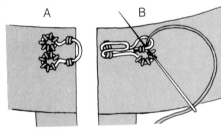

A   B

Attaching at Edges That Overlap Use either two standard hooks with straight eyes or one waistband hook and eye and sew them on as follows:

1. *Place the hook on the side of the garment that will become the overlap, about ¼" (6mm) from the edge. Sew through all the holes to secure the hook.*

2. *Lap the garment edges and* mark the position of the eye on the underlap by placing a pin where the end of the hook lines up (A). Attach the straight eye by sewing through both the holes (B).

3. *If you are using two standard hooks with straight eyes, the hooks and eyes should be positioned one above the other (C).*

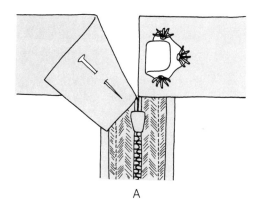

A

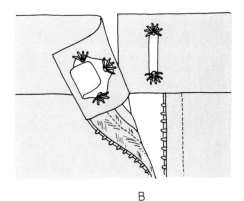

B

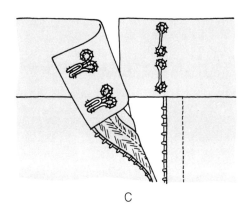

C

Interfacing

Interfacing adds shape to your garment and provides support in areas that are subject to extra stress. It helps create and maintain the smooth roll required in areas such as collars, cuffs and lapels, and also reinforces and stabilizes detail areas such as necklines, facings, pockets, waistbands and buttonholes.

Your pattern includes pieces and instructions for interfacing crucial areas of the garment. Depending on your choice of fabric and the overall look you wish to achieve, you may decide to interface other areas, such as the sleeve hem and hemline of a winter coat.

CHOOSING THE RIGHT INTERFACING

Interfacings differ according to their stretchability.

▶ *Stable interfacings do not stretch in any direction. They give a crisp look to the finished garment. Nonwoven stable interfacings may be cut out in any direction.*

▶ *Interfacings with crosswise stretch give across their width, but are stable in the lengthwise direction. These provide a softer effect than stable interfacings.*

▶ *All-bias interfacings stretch in any direction. Therefore, they can be cut out in any direction. These interfacings provide a hand (technical term for drape and feel of a fabric) that is as soft, or softer, than the crosswise-stretch interfacings.*

Which interfacing you use depends on your choice of fashion fabric and the area to be interfaced, as well as the total picture you wish to achieve. Although most interfacings are general-purpose ones, some are designed for specific areas, such as waistbands, straight facings, shirt plackets and cuffs.

Most often, the interfacing you choose should be slightly lighter in weight than your fashion fabric. In the case of fusible interfacings, the only way to be absolutely sure you like the way fabric and interfacing interact is to *test-fuse a small piece of the interfacing to your fashion fabric.* Although a fusible and a sew-in interfacing may appear to be the same when you drape them over your hand, the effect will be slightly crisper when a fusible type is applied to fabric.

Select an interfacing color that blends with the fabric—*dark interfacings for dark colors and white or beige interfacings for light colors.* Besides being aesthetically pleasing, you won't have to worry about the interfacing showing through to the outside of the garment. In addition, if the buttonhole area is interfaced, contrasting threads won't be a problem once the buttonholes are cut open. There are several interfacings that come in an assortment of fashion colors. These are designed for lightweight and sheer fabrics—pick the color that is closest to your fabric.

Every interfacing is labeled with care information. Read it carefully—your fabric and interfacing should have compatible care requirements. You wouldn't want to put a "dry-clean-only" interfacing in a child's garment that you intend to wash.

APPLYING

Woven, nonwoven and knitted interfacings are all available as fusible or sew-in types. Although fusing is usually considered the faster method, it still takes time, even if it is spent at the ironing board rather than at the sewing machine. The choice between a fusible and a sew-in interfacing is often a matter of personal preference.

Sew-In This type of interfacing is usually basted in place, then permanently machine stitched into the garment during the construction process. These interfacings are suitable for any type of fabric.

Sew-in interfacings are usually applied directly to the body of the garment, not to the facing, and to the outside of waistbands and cuffs. On collars, the interfacing is applied to either the upper or under collar, depending on the type of garment and the reason for using interfacing. If it is used to provide support, the interfacing is applied to the upper collar; if it is used for shaping, the interfacing is applied to the under collar.

Cut out the interfacing, making sure that the pattern pieces are laid out on-grain or according to the interfacing's stretchability (A). Pin or glue baste the interfacing in place on the wrong side of the garment section, matching seamlines and markings. Machine baste or staystitch ½" (13mm) from the edge (B). Trim the interfacing close to the stitching (C) and proceed with your pattern instructions.

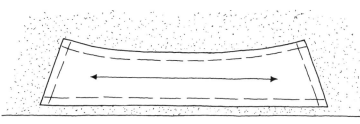

A

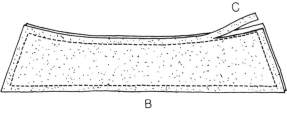

B

If you are applying interfacing to a garment section with a foldline along one edge, such as a collar, a cuff, a waistband or an edge with an extended facing, the way you treat that folded edge depends on how the garment is constructed.

To cut out lightweight or sheer fusible interfacings, place the interfacing fabric over the pattern piece and trace just outside the seamline, on the seam allowance. Cut out the interfacing sections along the traced lines.

▶ *If the edge will be top-stitched or edgestitched, trim the interfacing off right at the foldline, then secure it along the foldline with a hemming stitch (D).*

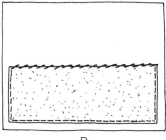

D

▶ *If the edge will not be top-stitched or edgestitched, cut out the interfacing so that it extends approximately ½" (13mm) beyond the foldline. Secure it to the garment section along the foldline with long running stitches spaced about ½" (13mm) apart, with only a tiny, invisible stitch catching the garment fabric (E).*

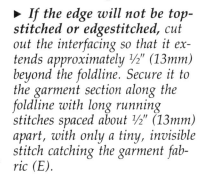

E

119

Fusible You'll recognize this type of interfacing by a shiny resin coating on one side. It's the coating that melts and bonds the interfacing to the fabric. Never put a fusible interfacing into your garment without test-fusing first. The result may be softer or crisper than you expected and, once the two are fused together, it's too late to change your mind. There are some fabrics—rayon and acetate velvets, fake furs, synthetic leathers, openwork lace and mesh, rainwear, textured brocades and heat-set plissés—that are not suitable for fusible interfacings.

Fusible interfacing is fused directly to the facing section, rather than to the body of the garment. This reduces the possibility that the outline of the interfacing will show on the outside. It is also fused to the upper collar, rather than the undercollar, and to the outside layer of waistbands and cuffs.

When using a fusible interfacing, always preshrink your fashion fabric. If you don't, the first time the completed garment is washed, the fabric may shrink but the interfacing won't. As a result, the interfaced areas will be distorted.

All fusible interfacings are sold with directions for cutting out and applying them. Cut out the interfacing sections, taking into account any grainlines or stretchability. If your pattern does not include separate pattern pieces for the interfacing, use the garment sections, trimming off ½" (13mm) from all seam allowances after cutting.

For detail areas with foldlines, see Sew-In Interfacing, pages 118–19.

Pin the interfacing, coated side down, on the wrong side of the garment section, matching seamlines and markings. Steam baste it in position with the tip of your iron, pressing lightly at a few points around the edges (A). Remove the pins, then fuse the interfacing into position permanently (B).

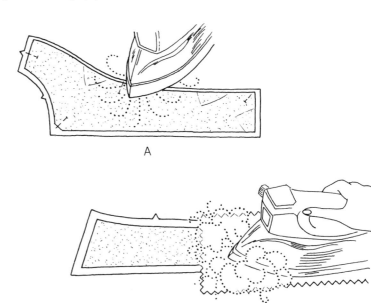

A

B

A good bond between fabric and interfacing is the key to successfully using fusible interfacing. Read the manufacturer's fusing directions carefully and follow them. Some recommend a combination of pressure, a *dry* iron and a *damp* press cloth, while others recommend pressure, a *steam* iron and a *dry* press cloth.

Keep in mind that pressure is as important as heat. Today's lightweight irons are not always heavy enough to provide sufficient pressure for a strong bond. You must supply the missing weight by leaning heavily on your iron. Never slide your iron as you move it from place to place. Lift it, overlapping it throughout the area (C).

side of the garment section. This produces a strong, even bond, reducing the possibility of missed spots. Let the fabric cool, then check the bond. If there are still any missed spots, repeat the fusing procedure in these areas for an additional 5 to 10 seconds.

The buttonhole area, particularly on children's garments, often needs extra reinforcement. If the facing for this part of the garment is not already interfaced, fuse a small patch of interfacing at each buttonhole position. Cut the patches out with pinking shears so there won't be a defined straight edge showing through to the outside of the garment (D).

If your iron doesn't seem to be providing sufficient heat and steam to get a good bond, try putting a piece of aluminum foil on your ironing board, underneath all the layers to be fused, so that it serves as a reflective surface.

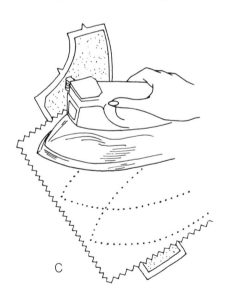

C

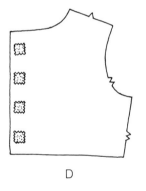

D

Even if the fusing directions do not suggest it, it's always a good idea to go through the fusing process twice, first on the wrong side, then on the right

For more information:

on Glue Stick, Machine and Pin Basting, see under BASTING.

on Hemming and Running Stitch, see under HAND SEWING.

on Edgestitching and Topstitching, see under MACHINE STITCHING.

Machine Stitching

Sewing machines have come a long way from the days of the treadle-operated, straight-stitch machines. Many of today's conventional sewing machines can zigzag, overcast, blindstitch, embroider, monogram and sew on any fabric from the sheerest voile to the thickest fake fur.

Computerized machines are the Cadillacs of the sewing industry. You can program these machines to sew variations of the built-in stitches, either singly or in a specified sequence for an embroidered effect; to monogram initials; or to stitch a series of perfectly identical buttonholes—all at the touch of a button or two.

Some machines do your thinking for you. Just press one set of buttons to describe your fabric and another set for your sewing procedure and the machine automatically determines the proper stitch, stitch length and width, indicates the correct presser foot and adjusts the tension.

Consult your manual for a listing of the stitches your sewing machine produces automatically and those it can produce with the turn of a dial or the addition of an accessory. Become familiar with these stitches by taking the time to practice them on scraps of various fabrics. Keep scraps of your fashion fabric by your side as you sew to test out any new stitch before you use it on your child's garment, since different weights of fabrics often require stitch length and width adjustments.

There are certain conventional machine sewing techniques and terms that are standard, regardless of the complexity of your machine.

Backstitching This technique is used to secure the stitches at the beginning or end of a seam. Essentially, you are sewing backward for several stitches.

To backstitch at the beginning of a seam, insert the needle along the seamline, approximately ⅜" (10mm) from the edge of the seam. Sew in reverse until you reach the edge of the fabric, then sew forward, exactly over the previous stitches, until you come to the end of the seam. Put the machine into reverse and sew four or five stitches to secure the end of the seam.

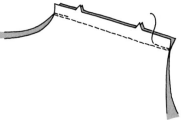

Easestitching Easing is the process of creating shape in a garment to match a body curve by joining one layer of fabric to another slightly smaller layer. Your pattern tells you when and where to ease, and provides you with matching points to ensure that the layers are joined accurately.

An easestitch is the same elongated machine stitch that is used to create gathers.

1. *Set your machine to a fairly long stitch, about 6 to 8 stitches per inch (per 2.5cm). Stitch along the seamline of the longer section only, between the markings. Leave long thread ends and do not secure the ends of your stitching.*

2. *Pin the two layers together, matching all marking points.*

3. *Pull the fabric up on the bobbin thread, as you would to gather, evenly distributing the fullness and smoothing out any tucks. Pin baste or machine baste to hold the ease evenly, then stitch the garment sections together along the seamline.*

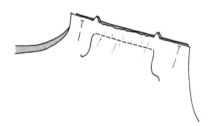

Edgestitching The name of the stitch tells you what is happening. You stitch very close to a finished or folded edge to keep all layers in place and to prevent the seam joining two fabric layers from rolling to the outside of the garment. The result is a clean, flat appearance. Edgestitching is considered a decorative feature on sporty or tailored garments, particularly on pockets, plackets, pleats, necklines, armholes, collars, lapels and hems. It can also be used to permanently secure pants leg or pleat creases. Edgestitching should be used in combination with, but never as a substitute for, proper pressing techniques.

1. *For better control, use the small hole throat plate because soft fabrics would be pulled into the larger, general-purpose throat plate opening. Unless your machine has a special foot for edgestitching, use the straight-stitch foot.*

2. *Stitch in a smooth line as close as possible to the finished or folded edge, following the natural edge of the garment section.*

3. *If you have a straight-stitch foot with one small toe, position the inside right edge of this toe along the folded edge of the fabric as you stitch. If you use a multi-purpose foot, position it close to the folded edge as you stitch.*

Overcasting The meaning of this term depends upon whether you do your sewing on a standard sewing machine or on an overlock machine.

The stitch pattern varies from machine to machine. Some standard sewing machines produce a stitch that closely resembles the overlock machine stitch; others produce a stitch that forms a honeycomb pattern; others produce a slanted, over-the-edge stitch. What some manuals refer to as an overlock stitch others call a knit stitch, emphasizing its built-in elasticity. Become familiar with your machine and its terminology! In general, this stitch is suitable for both knits and wovens.

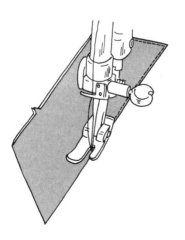

1. *To use this stitch as a seam finish on a plain seam, overcast the edges before, or after, the seam is sewn. Because children's clothes have many small detail areas, you will probably find it easier to finish the seams first, then sew the garment sections together.*

2. *To join and overcast a seam with the overcast stitch, trim the seam allowance to the width of the stitch, pin or glue baste the layers together (being careful to keep the glue within the narrow seam allowance) and stitch.*

Reinforcement Stitching Use this straight stitch to strengthen an area that will be subject to stress. The reinforcement may be done by adding an extra row of stitches before, or after, the seam is sewn or by shortening the stitch length as you sew.

If a corner must be clipped before it is joined to another section, reinforce it by stitching just inside the seamline, on the seam allowance, for about 1" (2.5cm) on either side of the corner. Clip to the point (A). Pin

both sections with right sides together and the clipped section up. Stitch the seam, pivoting at the point (B).

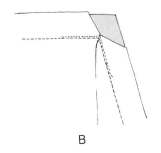

B

When an area will be closely trimmed before it is turned, such as an inside corner, reinforce the corner as the seam is sewn by shortening the stitches for about 1" (2.5cm) on either side of the corner (C).

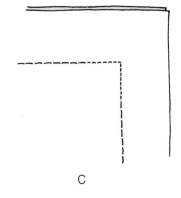

C

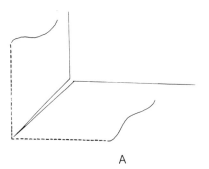

A

Areas subject to strain, such as an underarm or a crotch seam, are reinforced with an extra row of stitching after the seam is sewn. This second line of stitching should be placed on top of the original stitching or just next to it, on the seam allowance (D).

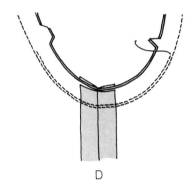

D

Staystitching This is done to stabilize garment pieces in bias or very curved areas. When used as a guideline for seams that need to be clipped, it helps stop you from cutting beyond the seam allowance. Staystitching should be done immediately after you remove the pattern tissue from the fabric. Otherwise, even the gentlest handling may distort the shape.

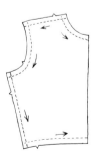

1. *Stitch ⅛" (3mm) from the seamline, on the seam allowance. Because most seam allowances are ⅝" (15mm), this distance is usually ½" (13mm) from the raw edge.*

2. *Stitch slowly, guiding the fabric lightly with your fingers. Don't pull on the fabric or you will distort its shape. Leave small thread ends (about ½" or 13mm long) and do not secure the ends of the stitching.*

3. *Place the pattern tissue against the area you have staystitched to make sure both are still identical. If not, gently pull the bobbin thread to readjust the staystitched area.*

Topstitching Like edgestitching, topstitching is one or more rows of stitching placed a desired distance from a finished edge. As a decorative finish, it emphasizes the structural lines of a garment. As a functional finish, farther away from an edge than edgestitching, it takes the place of edgestitching, keeping seams flat and edges from rolling to the outside of the garment.

To determine the best stitch length and thread tension for your project, experiment on a double layer of your fabric scraps. Although topstitching is usually done with a straight stitch that is 6 to 8 stitches per inch (per 2.5cm), on children's garments consider topstitching with a decorative stitch.

Topstitching can be done after the garment is completed. Or, if you are using the Flat Construction Method, topstitch each garment section, where possible, while it is still flat.

Working with the right side of the garment section facing up, stitch where indicated by your pattern instructions, using a guide to maintain a straight line of stitches.

Topstitching is often placed ¼" (6mm) from the edge or seam. To do this without measuring, place the outside edge of the right toe of your presser foot along the edge or seam (A).

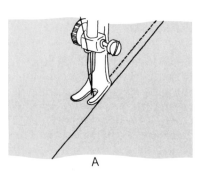

A

If you will be topstitching more than ¼" (6mm) away from the edge, apply sewing tape along the topstitching line as a guide, being careful not to stitch through the tape (B).

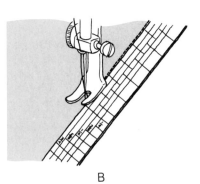

B

Understitching When a facing, a lapel or the edge of a collar just won't stay flat, and edge-stitching or topstitching is inappropriate, understitching is an alternative to get the control you need.

1. *Once the seam allowances are graded and clipped, open out the facing and press the facing and the seam allowances away from the body of the garment.*

2. *Working on the right side of the facing, machine stitch close to the seamline, through all the seam allowances (C).*

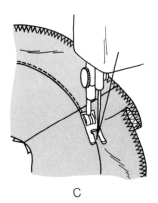

C

3. *Fold the facing to the inside of the garment and press.*

Zigzag Stitching This durable stitch has many uses. By varying the length and width of the stitch, you can use zigzag stitching to finish seams (A), to sew elastic directly to a garment, to create a machine-made buttonhole, to understitch bulky fabrics or to mend a rip or a tear in a garment.

The blindstitch used for hemming is a variation of the zigzag stitch (B).

A satin stitch, a zigzag stitch with a very short stitch length, is used for machine embroidery and appliqué (C).

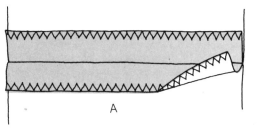

A

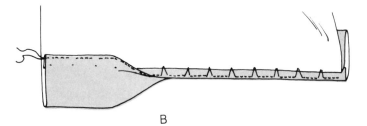

B

C

Nylon Hook and Loop Tape

Nylon hook and loop tape is one of the easiest fasteners to use. It's simple for you to apply to a garment and easy for little fingers to manipulate. Although there are several different manufacturers of this tape, it is most commonly known as Velcro.

The tape consists of two parts: the *hook* section with densely spaced nylon hooks and the *loop* section with a fuzzy, soft, velour-like surface. To close the two sections, press them together. To separate them, just pull them apart.

Nylon hook and loop tape is particularly suitable for children's casual wear. Because the tape is soft and flat, it's comfortable against a child's body. Unlike snaps, buttons and standard hooks and eyes, you needn't worry that the fastener will fall off the garment and end up in a baby's mouth, or separate from the garment because of frequent launderings. And, since it's an easy fastener to use, it's perfect for young children who are learning to dress.

Nylon hook and loop tape does have some limitations. It's not a good choice for tight-fitting garments—too much stress and strain will cause the tape to pop open. It's also not suitable for very lightweight fabrics, where the tape would be too bulky. In addition, because the line of stitching for the loop section is visible on the outside of the garment, you may not want it for dressy clothing.

Nylon hook and loop tape is available in various widths, shapes, colors and weights. It can be purchased in strips by the yard; it is also packaged in precut strips, dots, circles and squares. Use the strips as closures on long garment sections in place of a zipper or a row of buttons. Use the small shapes for spot closures, such as at the neckline or on a cuff.

Some tapes are self-basting, with adhesive on the back of each section. Simply press them into position and they will stay until you attach them permanently. If the tape you choose is not self-basting, use pins, basting tape or a dot of glue stick to hold the tape in place for stitching.

Because the hook side is rough, always position it on the underlap so it will be facing away from the body.

1. *To prevent the tape from showing when the garment is closed, the amount you allow for an underlap and an overlap should be wider than the tape. Place the hook section on the underlap and stitch around all the edges, through the tape and the layers of fabric.*

2. *Place the loop section, fuzzy side down, over the hook section. Position the overlap on top of the tape as if the garment were closed and mark or check the placement lines for the loop section. Separate the two sections.*

3. *Align the loop section of the tape on the overlap and pin or baste it in place. Stitch around all the edges, through the tape and the layers of fabric.*

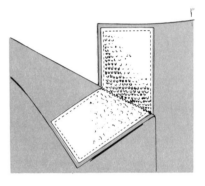

When washing garments with hook and loop tape, always close the tape to keep the hook side from snagging other garments or attracting bits of laundry lint.

For more information:

on Basting Tape, Glue Stick and Pin Basting, see under BASTING.

Overlock Stitching

A revolutionary addition to the homemaking scene is the overlock machine, which stitches, trims and overcasts a seam at the same time. This machine has technical capabilities which are faster and slightly different from those on the standard sewing machine. This section includes basic overlock sewing information. You'll also find tips and techniques for using overlock stitching included in many of the other methods in the Construction Techniques section. The overlock machine is comparable to a food processor. Just as there are some mixing procedures your food processor can't do, there are some sewing procedures you can't perform on an overlock machine. Both, however, can simplify your life enormously.

In one step, an overlock machine trims, joins and overcasts a seam; or trims and finishes the edge of the fabric. And it does this at about 1,500 stitches per minute—twice as fast as the conventional sewing machine. The stitching process is generally referred to as serging and you may hear the machine called a serger. The stitch that is created is referred to as an overcast, overedge or overlock stitch, depending upon the manufacturer. An overlock machine cannot make traditional straight, zigzag or embroidery stitches. You will still need your conventional machine to stitch a standard seam, insert a zipper, stitch buttonholes, topstitch and do decorative work.

As you become familiar with overlock machines, you learn a new sewing machine vocabulary. An overlock machine has either one or two needles (A) and one or two upper threads. Instead of bobbins, however, it has one or two lower parts called *loopers* and one or two lower threads. If there are two loopers, one is called an *upper looper* (B), the other, a *lower looper* (C). The blade that trims the excess seam allowance just before it is overlocked is called a *cutter* or a *knife* (D). The two tiny prongs just in front of the needle on the presser foot are called *stitch fingers* (E). The thread tension is controlled by a series of dials or disks (F).

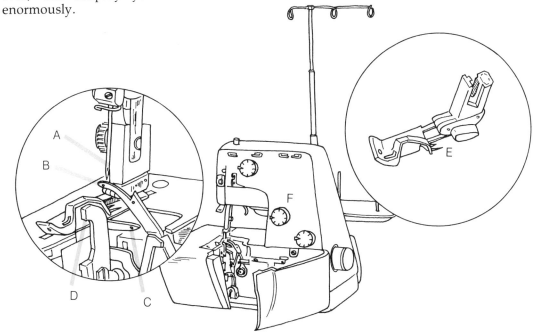

129

MACHINE TYPES

There are several different types of overlock machines that perform different functions, depending upon the number of threads and needles. No one machine does it all, so the right one for you depends on the type of sewing you want to do.

▶ The **two-thread** overlock machine, with one needle and one looper, is primarily a finishing machine. The overedge stitch it forms resembles the overcast stitch done on many conventional sewing machines (A). Seams can be finished on the two-thread machine either before or after they are sewn on a standard machine.

A two-thread overlock does a decorative "flatlock" joining seam which is perfect for T-shirts and sweatshirts. To make a flatlock seam, place the two fabric layers wrong sides together and overlock a seam. Then pull the layers apart so the overlocked edges lie flat between the stitching (B). Because the raw edges are somewhat exposed, the flatlock seam cannot be used on a fabric that ravels easily.

Some two-thread overlock machines will also do a narrow rolled hem.

▶ The **three-thread** overlock machine has one needle and two loopers. It can be used to finish an edge, to create a narrow rolled hem or to trim, join and overcast a seam (C). It creates a strong seam with built-in stretch that is particularly useful for knits, including swimwear and activewear. Although the stitch is suitable for all fabrics, it's not a good choice for a seam that is under a great deal of stress, such as the crotch seam on a pair of overalls, unless you add a row of conventional machine stitches. Some three-thread machines convert to two-thread machines, so that it is also possible to flatlock a seam.

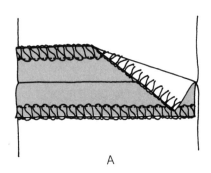

A

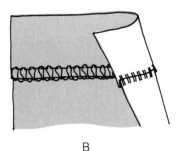

B

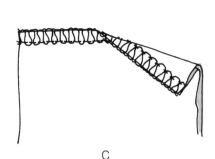

C

▶ A ***three/four-thread*** *overlock machine has two needles and two loopers. The extra needle and thread form a safety stitch down the middle of the looper threads to reinforce a seam or strengthen ravel-prone raw edges (D). Use this stitch with confidence on all knits and wovens. To convert it to a three-thread model, simply remove one of the needles.*

▶ *The true **four-thread** overlock uses two threads to create an overedge finish and two threads to create a chainstitch to the left of the overedge (E). Because the resulting seam is very strong but* not very stretchy, it is not a good choice for knit fabrics. You can convert the machine to sew just an overedge finish for seams, or just a chainstitched seam that can be easily removed. True four-thread overlocks cannot sew a narrow rolled hem.

SELECTING THREAD

Any type of thread can be used on the overlock machine as long as it is a strong, fine-quality thread. Because the thread travels through many thread guides at a rapid speed, strength is crucial. Avoid the "discount" threads with thick and thin spots that will affect stitch uniformity and make the thread snap.

Any fiber content is suitable—100 percent cotton (on wovens but not on knits because of its limited stretch), 100 percent polyester, cotton-wrapped polyester, nylon, rayon or silk. Because the overlock machine uses great quantities of thread, many manufacturers are now making their product available in large bulk spools or cones. The thread on these spools is crosswound so it slips off the spool easily when the machine is sewing at a high speed (F).

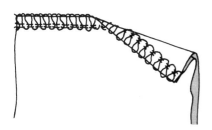

D

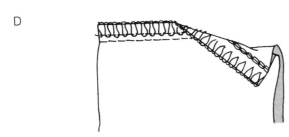

E

F

For special decorative effects, use pearl cotton, crochet thread, lightweight yarn or $1/16''$–$1/8''$ (2–3mm) ribbon in the loopers.

BEFORE YOU SEW

Because the overlock machine operates at a high speed, and because it trims while it stitches, you must adapt some of your sewing procedures accordingly.

Marking As the machine trims and finishes a raw edge, it cuts

131

off the notches. If you choose to finish your fabric edges before seaming them, use a water soluble or air erasable marking pen (pretested on a scrap of your fabric) to indicate the position of notches and to mark other construction symbols.

Pinning While sewing over pins is *never* recommended, the action of the cutting knife makes it impossible on an overlock machine. As an alternative to pinning, use glue stick or basting tape placed on the part of the seam allowance that will be trimmed off. Either of these alternatives is essential when you are working with a fabric that must be matched, such as a stripe or a plaid, or with a slippery fabric. If you *must* use pins, place them to the left of the seamline, either horizontally or vertically.

Seam Guides Since many overlock machines do not come with an optional stitching guide, how are you going to know if you are sewing the seam accurately? The best way is to create your own seam guide.

1. *Using a toothpick or a pin, place a tiny dot of nail polish or paint on the very front of the presser foot, in a direct line with the needle(s) to indicate where the needle(s) penetrate(s) the fabric (G).*

2. *Mark guidelines for stitching a seam with a ⅜" (10mm) and a ⅝" (15mm) seam allowance on the dust plate cover. Put a piece of masking tape on the cover; then measure to the right, from the needle to the plate cover and mark with paint, nail polish or a*

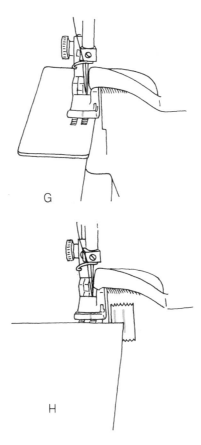

G

H

ball-point pen (H). Just be sure you measure from the needle, not from the space between the needle and the knife.

If a snap-on throat plate with marked lines is available for your machine, or if there are guidelines imprinted on the dust plate cover, you will not need to create the second set of markings.

There is another good reason for a seam guide. When you sew, the seam or fabric edge is always to the right of the needle. If you look carefully, you will see that there is a small clearance between the needle and the knife. If you position the fabric so that the edge glides along in

that space, you can use certain overlock techniques without cutting or trimming the edge.

SEWING BASICS

All overlock machines are not alike. You may need to adapt some of these techniques to your specific machine. Check your manual for further information.

Since there is very little space to juggle fabric, use Flat Construction Methods wherever possible. As a rule of thumb, use a narrow stitch width for lightweight to mediumweight fabrics and a wider stitch width for mediumweight to heavyweight fabrics. Certain techniques may also require changing the stitch length.

Starting a Seam Before you insert the fabric under the presser foot, run a 2" (5cm)-long chain of stitches. Then, with the fabric in place, bring the chain end to the left, around the needle(s), and place it on the seam allowance, slightly to the right of the needle(s). Secure the chain by stitching over the fabric *and* the chain for about 1" (2.5cm) (A).

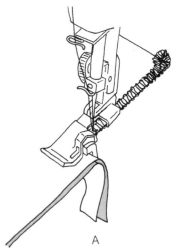

A

To trim off the excess chain, loop it in front of the knife; it is cut off as you continue to stitch.

Ending a Seam Although the stitches within the chain are tightly locked, loose threads and chains can make the inside of a garment look messy. To eliminate this, run a 2″ (5cm)-long chain of thread at the end of the seam and do one of the following:

▶ *Clip the chain close to the end of the seam and apply a drop of seam sealant, such as Fray Check (B).*

▶ *Thread a large-eyed needle with the chain and weave the chain back between the stitches (C).*

▶ *Tie the chain in a knot close to the edge of the fabric and trim the excess threads.*

▶ *Encase the end of the seam in extra stitches. To do this, stitch one stitch beyond the seam edge. Then lift the presser foot and carefully pull the threads off the stitch fingers. Turn the fabric over and position it in front of the needle. Restitch the end of the seam for 1″ (2.5cm) and then stitch off the edge at a sharp angle (D). Knot the tail or secure with seam sealant.*

▶ *For circular shapes such as skirt hems, stop stitching with the needle in the fabric, raise the presser foot and fold the fabric back to the left so it is out of the way of the needle. Lower the presser foot, and continue stitching, angling these stitches away from the fabric (E). Either trim off the excess chain or weave it back between the stitches.*

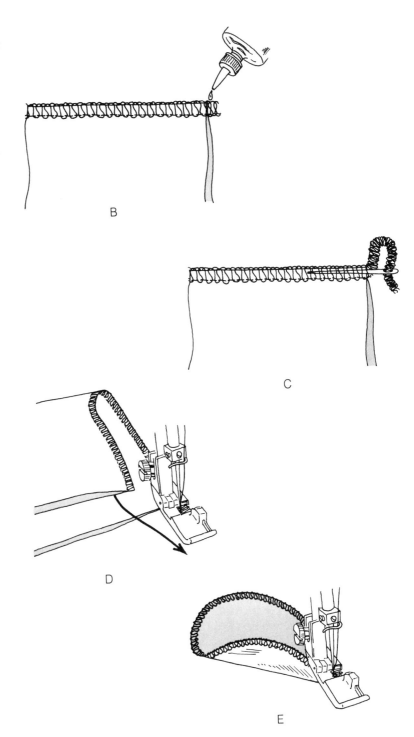

B

C

D

E

133

Safety Seams Seams that are subject to stress, particularly on children's play clothes, may require a second row of safety stitches done on your conventional sewing machine.

On shoulders and sleeves, overlock stitch the seam, press the seam allowances to one side and reinforce them by topstitching close to the seamline, through all thicknesses. On crotch and underarm seams, put the reinforcement stitches just outside the overlocked seam.

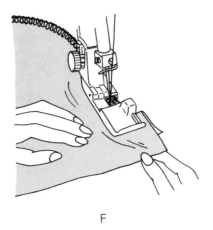

F

Curves The key to smooth curves is to maneuver the fabric so it is as straight as possible when you stitch. Since the knives and feed dogs on an overlock machine exert more pressure than on a standard sewing machine, use both hands to push or pull the fabric.

On *outside curves*, keep the flow of the fabric even by gently pulling the fullness toward the presser foot (F).

On *inside curves*, keep the flow of the fabric even by gently pushing the fullness toward the presser foot (G).

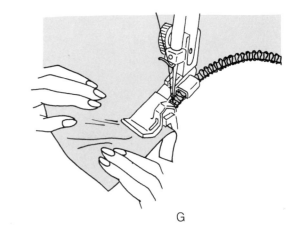

G

Corners Turning a corner on an overlock machine is a bit tricky. Practice these techniques several times before trying them on a garment.

On *inside corners*, mark both the stitching and the cutting lines with a water soluble or air erasable marker (tested first on your fabric) for 1" (2.5cm) on either side of the corner. Clip to the corner (H). Overlock stitch one edge until the knife reaches

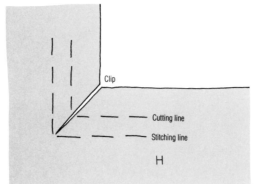

Clip

Cutting line

Stitching line

H

the cutting line for the other edge of the corner (I). Straighten out the fabric in front of the knife and continue overlock stitching along the other side of the corner (J).

On *outside corners,* pretrim the fabric to the finished size. Overlock to the tip of the corner, stitching one stitch past the point. Gently pull the thread chain from the stitch fingers (K). Turn the fabric, realign it under the presser foot with the edge of the throat plate and continue stitching (L). When you reach the last corner, secure the stitches, using one of the finishing methods explained earlier.

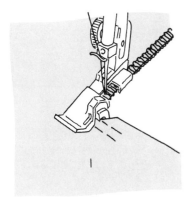

I

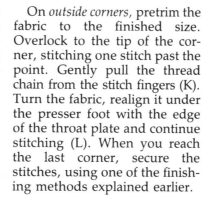

K

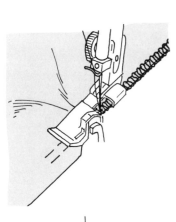

J

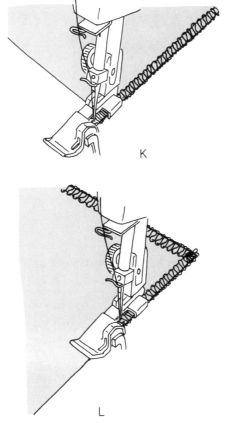

L

135

Ripping Out Stitches As a general rule, ripping out stitches should be avoided whenever possible because your stitches are "locked" in and the seam allowance is trimmed away. If you *must* rip, here's how to do it for each type of overlock machine:

▶ *Two-thread overlock:* Use a seam ripper to cut the stitches (A), then pull out the threads.

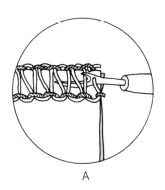

A

▶ *Three-thread and three/four-thread overlock:* On the top side of the stitching, clip the needle thread(s) at every third or fourth stitch (B). Grasp both looper threads at the edge of the stitching and pull to remove (C). Then pull out the needle thread(s).

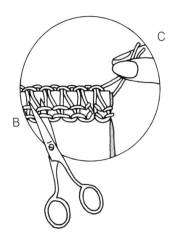

▶ *Four-thread overlock: On the bottom side of the stitching, pull on the looper thread at the end of the chainstitching (D). It may be necessary to pull out one or more loops to release the chain. Then use a seam ripper to cut the overedge stitches (E); pull out the cut threads.*

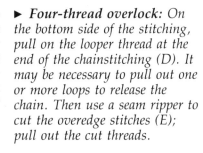

Pleats

Pleats add fullness and a special sense of style to children's garments. Simple, inverted pleats provide the necessary room and comfort in clothes for toddlers and babies.

Pleats are essentially folds in the fabric. There are four common types of pleats. Each can be used singly or as a series in a garment.

▶ *Knife* or *side pleats* have all the folds turned in one direction.

▶ *Box pleats* have two folds turned away from each other so that the underfolds meet at the center.

▶ *Inverted pleats* are box pleats in reverse, with the folds turned toward each other so that they meet in the center on the outside of the garment.

▶ *Accordion pleats* are always pressed along the entire length of the fabric in narrow folds resem-bling the bellows of an accor-dion.

You can treat the pleat folds in a variety of ways:

▶ *Traditional pressed pleats* are folded and basted into place, then pressed along the entire length of the garment section to give each pleat a crisp, sharp edge.

▶ *Stitched pleats* are pressed and edgestitched along the length of the garment section.

▶ *Stitched-and-released pleats* are pressed along the length of the garment section, then edgestitched or topstitched for a specified distance.

▶ *Unpressed pleats* are folded and basted into place along the length of each pleat and across the top of the pleats, then steamed lightly so that each pleat has a soft, rounded edge.

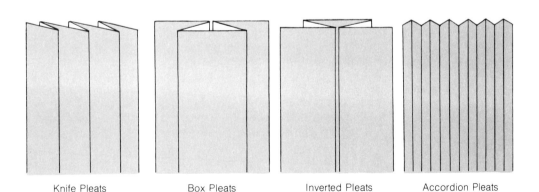

Knife Pleats   Box Pleats   Inverted Pleats   Accordion Pleats

MARKING PLEATS

For precise results, transfer the pleat construction lines indicated on your pattern tissue to your fabric with care.

For unpressed pleats, one or more of these lines are identified as *roll lines*, as these pleats form soft, rolling folds. For pressed pleats, these lines are identified as *foldlines*, as they form a sharply creased fold. Patterns for both types of pleats also have construction lines called *placement lines* which the rolled or creased edges must meet to form the pleat.

Pleats can be marked and constructed from either the right or wrong side, depending on the style of the finished garment and your own personal preference. Mark pleats made from the right side on the right side of the fabric, and pleats made from the wrong side on the wrong side of the fabric.

Using tracing paper and a tracing wheel is probably the easiest, most efficient, method of marking pleats. Use a different color tracing paper for foldlines or roll lines than for placement lines. If you are marking the right side of a washable fabric, use water soluble tracing paper, testing it first on a scrap of the fabric.

STITCHING

The basic method of folding and stitching the pleats remains the same whether the finished pleats are pressed or unpressed. It's best to do the pleating on a surface large enough to hold the entire pleated garment.

If you are sewing a skirt with a series of pressed pleats, hem it before making the pleats. Otherwise, you will have difficulty getting the pleats to lie flat in the hem area.

To construct pleats from the wrong side, turn the fabric in along the foldline or roll line and bring each folded edge to meet its corresponding placement line, matching all markings. Baste the layers together along the two lines (A). Press or turn pleats in the direction indicated for your type of pleat. Baste the pleats in place along the top edge.

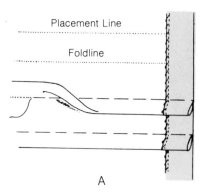

Placement Line

Foldline

A

To construct pleats from the right side, turn the fabric in along the foldline or roll line, then bring the folded edge to meet its corresponding placement line and pin the layers together along the lines. Starting at the hem edge and working upward, baste each pleat in place along the edge of the fold through all thicknesses (B). Baste the pleats in place along the top edge.

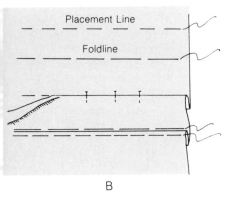

B

If you are making a pleated skirt for an older child, you may wish to have her try the pleated garment on to check the fit. Before you do, baste a temporary belt of grosgrain ribbon at the waistline on the inside. This will provide support so that the pleats will hang properly as you fit the garment.

If the waistline is too large or too small, distribute the change evenly among the pleats, making a hairline waist adjustment on the placement line of each pleat. On straight pleats, it is very important to maintain the straight grainline on the outside fold of each pleat by carefully tapering the adjustment to meet the placement line (C).

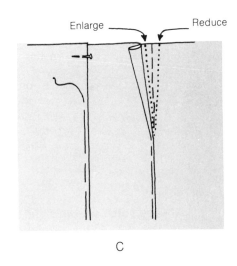

C

PRESSING

Pleats, whether they are crisp or soft, should be pressed before edgestitching or topstitching, as well as before attaching the pleated section to another section of the garment, such as a waistband or a bodice. See pages 43–44 for information about proper techniques for pressing pleats.

EDGESTITCHING AND TOPSTITCHING

Edgestitch or topstitch the pleats before joining the pleated section to another part of the garment.

Stitch close to the outside creased edge of each pleat, stitching from the hem up toward the waistline. For extra crispness and security, you may also wish to stitch the inside folds from the wrong side (A).

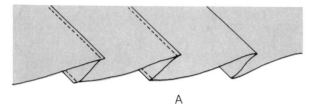

A

Topstitching Straight Pleats
Always stitch on the right side of the garment through all thicknesses. Stitch from the hip area up toward the waistline. Mark each pleat where the top-stitching begins.

For *knife* or *side pleats*, pin the pleats in place, then topstitch close to the edge of the fold (B).

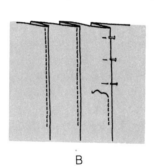

B

For *inverted pleats*, topstitch along both sides of the outside fold. Begin stitching where the folds meet, taking two or three stitches across the pleat, then pivoting and stitching to the waistline an even distance from the fold. Repeat, beginning where the folds meet and stitching up the side of the other fold (C). To secure the beginning of the stitching, pull the thread ends to the inside and tie.

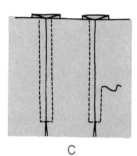

C

For more information:

on Edgestitching and Topstitching, see under MACHINE STITCHING.

on Marking Pleat Lines, see under WHAT TO KNOW BEFORE YOU SEW.

Pockets

Everyone needs pockets in their clothes, especially kids. Pockets are a great place to hoard a candy bar, stash tiny treasures, hide small toys from curious siblings or to transport something practical like a handkerchief.

PATCH POCKETS

Patch pockets are applied to the outside of children's clothes. They are the perfect place to show off a bit of patchwork, add an appliqué or embroider a monogram. Although most patch pockets are either square or have rounded bottom edges, these pockets can become quite whimsical, taking the shape of a heart, a building block or a watermelon wedge.

Study your fabric carefully before laying out the pattern pieces for a patch pocket. If it is a fabric with a nap, such as corduroy, or one with a one-way design, make sure the pocket is cut so that the nap or design is heading in the same direction on both the pocket and the garment sections.

Making a Template Cut, finish and stitch patch pockets identically so that the right and left side of each pocket forms a mirror image. In addition, pockets often come in twos—and the pair must be identical. This is easy to do if you make a pocket template from a piece of lightweight cardboard or fine sandpaper cut to the exact finished size and shape of the pocket. It's an invaluable shaping and pressing aid for both square and rounded unlined patch pockets.

Cut out the pocket sections. Use the pocket pattern piece to create a template, omitting the pocket facing and seam allowances.

Unlined Patch Pockets—Round

1. *The finished pocket should have a smoothly curved lower edge and an even, squared-off upper edge. To insure a perfect upper edge, transfer the foldline marking from the pocket pattern tissue to the fabric with chalk, marking pen or pencil.*

2. *Finish the upper edge of the pocket section, using the method most appropriate to your fabric. To make the pocket facing, fold the top edge along the foldline to the outside of the pocket. Press lightly along the fold.*

3. *Stitch around the sides and bottom of the pocket, just inside the seamline, on the seam allowance. Then easestitch along each curve on the right side, 1/4" (6mm) from the raw edge. Trim the seam allowance within the facing area only and diagonally trim the corners of the facing (A).*

4. *Turn the facing to the inside. Using a point turner (available at sewing notions counters), carefully push out the corners of the pocket. Press along the foldline of the facing.*

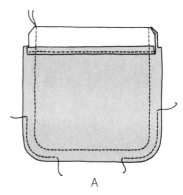

A

5. *If you are using a template, slip it under the facing so that the upper edge of the template is at the foldline. Fold the remaining seam allowances to the inside, over the template, so that the stitching lines roll to the inside. Pull up on the bobbin thread of the easestitching so that the edges curl over the template. If there is too much fullness at the curves, remove it by cutting off the ripples beyond the easestitching so the curved edge looks like it was clipped (B). Press the pocket edges.*

If you are not using a template, pull up on the bobbin thread of the easestitching so

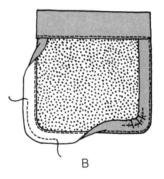

B

that the seam allowances curl toward the inside of the pocket. Press the pocket along the seamline, favoring the easestitching to the inside of the pocket as you press (C). If there is too much fullness at the curves, remove it as described previously.

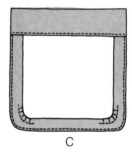

C

Unlined Patch Pockets—Square

1. *The finished pocket should have even, squared-off upper and lower edges. To ensure a perfect edge, transfer the foldline marking from the pocket pattern tissue to the fabric with chalk, marking pen or pencil.*

2. *Finish the upper edge of the pocket section, using the method most appropriate for your fabric. To create the pocket facing, fold the top edge along the foldline to the outside of the pocket. Press lightly along the fold.*

3. *Stitch around the sides and bottom of the pocket, just inside the seamline, on the seam allowance. Trim the seam allowances in the facing area only and diagonally trim the corners of the facing (A).*

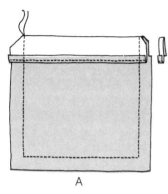

A

4. *Turn the facing to the inside and, using your point turner, carefully push out the corners of the pocket. Press along the foldline of the facing.*

5. *If you are using a template, slip it under the facing, with the upper edge of the template at the foldline. Fold the remaining seam allowances to the inside, over the template, so that the stitching lines roll to the inside. Press, mitering the bottom corners. If you are not using a template, roll the stitching lines to the inside, press, miter the corners and press again (B).*

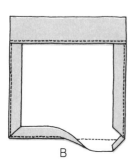

B

Applying Patch Pockets If you originally transferred your pattern markings to the wrong side of your fabric, now transfer these markings to the right side to know where to put the pockets. You can do this easily by inserting a pin at the marking point on the wrong side of the fabric through to the right side. If you want to remove the pins, mark the pinpoints with a water soluble or air erasable marking pen (tested first on a scrap of the fabric) or with tailor's chalk.

Before permanently securing the pockets to the garment, take the time to check the pocket position. Pin the pocket in place, step back and take a look. If you are sewing for an older child, or are not using the Flat Construction Method, consider applying the pocket near the end of the construction process, so you can check the garment length and pocket placement at the same time (C).

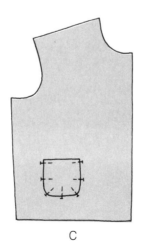

C

As an alternative to making a new template for each rounded patch pocket, you can purchase a pocket former template, a metal plate with four different rounded corners. A companion clip section holds the fabric in position over the curve as you press. To use the template, fold the seam allowances over the appropriate curve, insert the fabric and the template into the clip section and press. Repeat for the other curve.

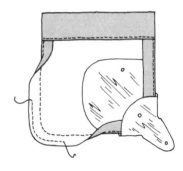

143

To make the pockets extra strong, reinforce them by stitching again over the first line of stitching, within the pocket area only.

Pockets should be conveniently located so that small arms can reach them easily. Because patch pockets are decorative, as well as functional, the placement should also be pleasing to the eye. If you have made any length or width adjustments on your garment, double-check the pocket placement to be sure it's in a usable and attractive position.

Because children are notoriously hard on their clothes, attach pockets securely with machine stitching on all but the most delicate finery. You will find it easier to apply pockets to flat garment sections wherever possible.

1. *Baste the pocket in place before permanently attaching it to the garment. Refer to Basting, pages 52–54, for techniques, or use one of the following methods:*

▶ *Use fusible web as you position the pocket on the garment. Place three narrow strips of web under the side and bottom edges of the pocket, about ⅛" (3mm) from the edge so that the web doesn't show.*

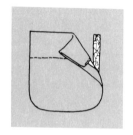

▶ *Use glue stick, applying a thin film along the seam allowances at the side and bottom edges of the pocket. Turn the pocket over, align it with the placement markings and press it firmly in place on the garment. Allow the glue to dry for a few minutes before stitching.*

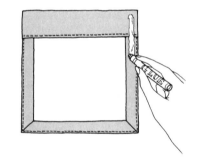

2. *Edgestitch or topstitch the pocket in place, depending upon the type of finish you have chosen for the rest of the garment. Reinforce the upper edges of the pockets to keep them from pulling out during wear. Begin stitching along one side of the pocket, about ½" (13mm) from*

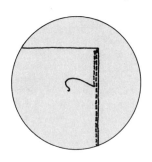

the upper edge. Backstitch until you reach the edge of the pocket, then stitch down the side, across the bottom and up the other side. When you reach the other upper corner, backstitch again for about ½" (13mm).

3. *For a tailored finish with extra reinforcement, add a second row of topstitching an equal distance from the first row. Use your presser foot as a guide to keep the two rows of stitching an even distance apart.*

IN-SEAM POCKETS

In adult garments, in-seam pockets are often constructed from a lightweight lining fabric. However, because most children are fond of stuffing things into their pockets, a sturdier fabric is usually a better choice. If the garment fabric is a suitable weight, use it. Otherwise, consider a lightweight, firmly woven fabric such as broadcloth.

For extra stability, add a stay along the seamline where the pocket is attached to the front of the garment. It reinforces the pocket edge and keeps it from stretching.

Constructing In-seam Pockets

1. *To construct the pocket stay, cut a piece of ribbon seam binding that is 2" (5cm) longer than the pocket opening. Working on the wrong side of the garment front, center the seam binding over the seamline along the pocket opening. Machine baste next to the seamline on the seam allowance (A).*

A

2. *With right sides together, join one pocket section to each side of the garment front, matching markings. Stitch in a ¼" (6mm) seam. Press the pocket and the seam allowances away from the garment front (B). Join the remaining pocket sections to the sides of the garment back.*

B

If you are worried about your topstitching being even, prepare and topstitch the pocket before attaching it to the garment. Next, baste the pocket in place on the garment and do one of the following:

■ Topstitch again, directly on top of the first row of topstitching, through the pocket and the garment section.

■ Edgestitch the pocket in place so that the finished pocket has two rows of stitching.

3. *With right sides together, baste the garment front to the garment back along the seamline. To permanently join the sections together, begin stitching at the lower edge of the garment section. Continue stitching around the pocket and along the upper edge of the garment section (C).*

4. *In order to make the garment seams lie flat, pull the pocket toward the front of the garment and clip only the back seam allowance, just above and just below the pocket. Press the seam open above and below the pockets (E).*

C

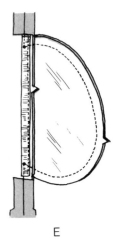

E

To maintain an even seam allowance at the upper and lower corners of the pocket, pivot your stitching at the pocket markings indicated on your pattern. Reinforce these pivot points by shortening the stitches (D).

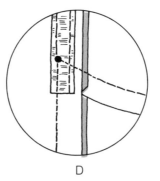

D

For more information:

on Pivoting, see under APPLIQUÉ.

see FUSIBLE WEB.

on Mitering, see under HEMS.

on Backstitching, Easestitching, Edgestitching, Overcasting, Reinforcement Stitching, Topstitching, and Zigzag Stitching, see under MACHINE STITCHING.

on Clipping, see under SEAMS.

on Finishing Edges, see under SEAM FINISHES.

on Transferring Markings, see under WHAT TO KNOW BEFORE YOU SEW.

Repairs

Children's clothes endure a great deal. With all the climbing, crawling, sliding and scooting that children do, tears, rips and snags are no strangers to their clothes. But a little skillfully applied first aid can make these clothes look as good as new. Patches sewn or fused in place are a popular form of camouflage. Bands of ribbon or lace may be edgestitched to disguise a tear. Machine darning is a good way to mend a hole or reinforce a worn spot. If the repair is in a suitable location, a patch pocket might be both a welcome addition and the perfect solution.

Before you decide how you are going to mend the garment, there are a few things you should consider.

▶ *Style. Dressy clothes require subtle mending, while play clothes can take more rugged repairs like machine darning or precut iron-on patches.*

▶ *Fabric. A self-fabric patch blends in better on textured or patterned fabrics than on solid or smooth fabrics. Ribbons and trims may be a more appropriate choice for soft, lightweight fabrics than patches or machine darning.*

▶ *Location. Worn elbows and knees should be mended with sturdy, no-nonsense patches in fabrics that resist further wear. Patch pockets and decorative appliqués should look like they were always part of the garment, not an afterthought.*

PATCHES

You can select self-fabric patches, almost invisible and strictly functional, covering up the hole, rip or tear without being noticed, or you can provide a touch of contrast in the form of a decorative appliqué. Create your own patches or use precut iron-on patches, prepackaged iron-on mending fabric or mending tape.

As a general rule, make the patch at least 1" (2.5cm) larger than the tear or hole in the garment.

Decorative For double duty, decorating and repairing a garment, you can't beat appliqués. Use simple, sturdy ones to mend elbows, knees and backsides. Save the delicate or fancy appliqués to repair the occasional rip that is not the result of normal wear and tear.

Before you conceal a tear or hole with an appliqué, cut a piece of fusible interfacing slightly larger than the hole and fuse it in place on the inside of the garment to keep the torn edges from fraying.

Self-Fabric If you've ever wondered why you save the leftover fabric from every sewing project, here's one time when you can certainly use it. When made from the same fabric as the original garment, the patch is almost invisible, particularly if the fabric is textured or patterned. If the fabric has a nap or a design that must be matched, such as a plaid or a stripe, cut the patch to match the garment section. Since this type of patch repairs, but does not reinforce, a worn area, don't use it in places that are subject to abrasion, such as elbows and knees. It's also not a good choice for lightweight and sheer fabrics.

Before you begin, compare a swatch of the leftover fabric with your garment. If the garment has faded so that the two are no longer the same color, you may wish to use another method.

In this method, the patch is machine stitched on the inside of the garment.

1. *Press the garment in the torn area, then cut away the rip or hole, forming a square or a rectangle. Reinforce the opening by machine stitching around it with a short stitch length, sewing ¼" (6mm) from the cut edges and pivoting at the corners. Clip the corner just to, but not through, the stitching line. Reinforce the corners and the cut edges with a liquid seam sealant, such as Fray Check (A).*

2. *Cut a self-fabric patch that is 1" (2.5cm) larger than the hole. Press the edges of the hole under ¼" (6mm), favoring the stitching line to the inside of the garment.*

3. *With right sides together, open out the pressed seam allowance and pin one edge of the hole to a corresponding edge of the patch. Working with the wrong side of the garment facing up, and starting at least 1" (2.5cm) from one corner, machine stitch along the creaseline until you come to the next corner (B). Pivot, then align the next edge*

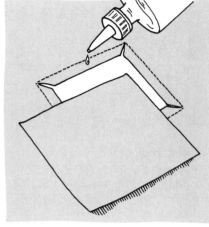

A

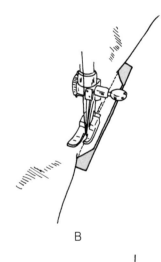

B

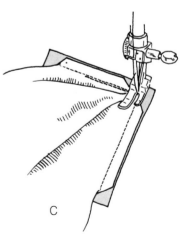

C

To repair snags and pulls in a jiffy, even while the child is wearing the garment, get yourself a Snag Nab-It™. This handy notion looks like a long, thin needle with tiny teeth on one end. Just insert the pointed end through the middle of the snag from the right side of the garment. As you pull the needle through the fabric, the "teeth" grab the snag and pull it through to the wrong side.

of the hole with the corresponding edge of the patch (C).

4. *Continue stitching and pivoting at the remaining corners until the stitching overlaps at the starting point. Press the patch so that the seam allowances are pressed away from the repaired area and toward the body of the garment.*

Iron-on For no-sew repairs, choose precut iron-on patches, mending fabric or mending tape.

Choose patches that are compatible with the color, texture, fiber content and care requirements of the garment. These patches, a popular choice for mending and reinforcing elbows and knees, create a casual, rugged effect when they contrast with the garment fabric. Once the patch is applied, you may wish to machine stitch around the outer edges using a satin stitch to keep the edges of the patch from curling up as a result of frequent launderings.

Iron-on mending fabrics and mending tapes are the same product, packaged in different ways. Mending fabric is precut into various-size rectangles that you can then cut into any size or shape you desire. Mending tape is sold in strips approximately 1¼" (3.2cm) wide. The choice between tape or fabric depends upon the size of the area you are covering up and whatever you find more convenient to use.

1. *Wash or dry-clean the garment before applying any of these mending aids.*

2. *Cut the fabric or tape 1" (2.5cm) larger than the hole or tear, rounding off any corners.*

3. *Warm the worn area by pressing with a dry iron.*

4. *Place the patch, coated side down, on the outside of the garment, cover with a press cloth and press, following the manufacturer's directions.*

TRICKS WITH TRIM

Sometimes the most effective way to cover a rip or a tear is to add one or more rows of trim to a garment. One row hides the hole; the additional rows create a balanced effect so that the trim looks like part of the garment. Use bands of ribbon, lace, braid, bias tape or other decorative trim as horizontal or vertical banding.

Cut down on repairs with preventive reinforcement on areas that receive hard wear, such as elbows and knees. Before you sew the garment together, cut a piece of fusible interfacing deep enough to cover the area and wide enough to extend into the side seams. To prevent a ridge from showing through on the outside of the garment, cut the piece with pinking shears. Fuse it in place, then sew the garment together according to the pattern instructions.

For more information:

see APPLIQUÉ.

on Satin Stitch, see under EMBROIDERY.

on Fusibles, see under INTERFACING.

on Reinforcement Stitching, see under MACHINE STITCHING.

Ribbons

You can use bands of ribbon to accent the design lines of a garment or to cover a telltale worn spot. Add a wide ribbon sash to make a basic dress party-special. Make ruffles from ribbons, eliminating the need to narrow hem the edges. Personalize a garment with hand embroidery, substituting ¹⁄₁₆" (2mm)-wide ribbon for the embroidery thread.

When you are looking for ribbons, select those with care requirements that are compatible with your fashion fabric. Machine-washable polyester ribbons, available in a range of styles from satins to velvets and grosgrains, are generally the best choice for children's clothes. Save the more expensive, "dry-clean-only" ribbons for some other sewing venture.

RIBBON TRIM

When you use ribbon trim, there are a few guidelines to follow.

▶ *The ribbon should be securely basted in place so that it doesn't slip out of position as you stitch. To baste, use glue stick or disappearing basting tape. If you are using basting tape, center it on the wrong side of the ribbon so you won't stitch through it when you sew the ribbon in place. Be careful not to press over the area before you remove the tape.*

▶ *Edgestitch the ribbon in place along both edges. To keep the ribbon from rippling, stitch both edges in the same direction.*

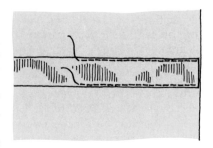

RIBBON RUFFLES

Ribbon ruffles are a quick and easy substitute for fabric ruffles. The ribbon's finished edge eliminates the need for making a hem. The ribbon should be permanent press or wrinkle resistant and at least 1½" (3.8cm) wide. If it is narrower, the finished ruffle won't lie smooth or flat.

To make the ruffle, cut the ribbon 2 to 2½ times the length of the edge to receive the ruffle. Gather one long edge of the ribbon ruffle and apply it to the edge of the garment, or encase it in a seam, following the procedures given in Ruffles, pages 151–53.

RIBBON EMBROIDERY

Ribbon gives a richly textured appearance to embroidery stitches. Use narrow, ¹⁄₁₆" (2mm)-wide ribbon as a substitute for embroidery thread. Almost any hand embroidery stitch, such as those described under Embroidery, pages 84–87, can be done with narrow ribbon. Keep these guidelines in mind when embroidering with ribbon.

▶ *To minimize twisting, use short lengths of ribbon—18" (46cm) or less.*

▶ *If the ribbon twists as you embroider, let the needle dangle free to unwind the ribbon, then continue.*

▶ *Sew with a #18 sharp or blunt needle, according to the fabric.*

▶ *To secure your embroidery at the beginning, make a tight knot in the ribbon, then bring the needle from the underside through to the upper side of the fabric. If you need to insert your needle back into the same hole, push the knot aside.*

▶ *To secure your ribbon embroidery at the end, insert the needle to the wrong side, weave it through the underside of several embroidery stitches, and then form a tight knot.*

For more information:

on Basting Tape and Glue Stick Basting, see under BASTING.

on Hand Gathering, see under GATHERING.

on Whipstitching, see under HAND SEWING.

on Edgestitching, see under MACHINE STITCHING.

see OVERLOCK STITCHING.

on Marking Placement Lines, see under WHAT TO KNOW BEFORE YOU SEW.

Ruffles

Designers use ruffles on children's clothes frequently as a decorative detail with soft, feminine fashion appeal. Narrow ruffles add a frilly touch; wide ones create a flounced effect.

Most fabric ruffles begin as long strips of fabric. If your pattern includes ruffles as a design feature, pattern pieces are provided. If you are creating your own ruffles, you need a strip of fabric that is two to three times the length of the garment section to receive the ruffle, depending on the ruffle fullness. You will also need to decide how wide the ruffle should be. Wide ruffles should have more fullness than narrower ones. The fabric you're using also affects the ruffle fullness; the more sheer the fabric, the fuller the ruffle should be. Another important consideration for children's clothing is the amount of pressing you'll have to do to maintain the garment. Permanent press or wrinkle-resistant fabrics are the most practical for carefree ruffles.

Make single- or double-layer ruffles, depending on the finished look you want. Single ruffles require a narrow hem finish and, because they are only one thickness, require less fabric. However, they are not suitable for fabrics that are printed only on one side, or have a definite right and wrong side. Double ruffles are made from a strip of fabric that is twice the total width of the finished ruffle plus two seam allowances. Because you don't need to finish the hem edge, double ruffles are faster and easier to make.

STRAIGHT GRAIN VS. BIAS

Ruffles can be cut on either the crosswise or lengthwise grain or on the bias. For easier patterns, ruffles are generally cut on the straight, usually crosswise, grain because they are easier to control during the hemming and gathering processes. Bias ruffles are more common on adults' clothes. They are a good choice for ruffles applied to a very curved garment edge. Bias ruffles are often cut double to eliminate the hem at the lower edge.

PIECING THE RUFFLE

To form a strip of fabric long enough to make a ruffle, piecing is often required. When it is necessary, your pattern cutting layout indicates the number of ruffle sections to cut. All the grainlines must match exactly. If the fabric has a nap, shading or a one-way design, be sure that you cut each section so that the entire ruffle matches.

With right sides together, stitch the ruffle sections at the short ends to form one long, continuous strip. Press the seam allowances open.

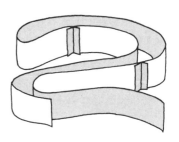

Use 1/16"- to 1/4" (2 to 6mm)-wide satin or grosgrain ribbon and your overlock machine to hem any garment edge. Set your machine to a stitch width that is slightly wider than the ribbon and long enough for the ribbon to show through. If your fabric tends to fray, make a test sample first to be sure the stitch secures the edge. Glue baste the ribbon on the right side of the garment along the hemline. Working with the ribbon facing up, stitch over it, cutting off the seam or hem allowance on the garment as you stitch. Be careful not to cut into the ribbon with the blade of the machine.

RUFFLES APPLIED TO AN EDGE

You'll find that both single and double ruffles can be attached to just about any garment edge, such as the lower edge of a sleeve or a skirt, a neckline or even a pocket.

Single This type of ruffle can be any width.

1. *Narrow hem one long edge of the ruffle (A). If the garment edge to receive the ruffle has an opening, narrow hem the remaining short ends of the ruffle. If the edge is a continuous circle, seam the remaining short ends.*

2. *To prepare the ruffle for gathering, stitch one row of long machine stitches at the seamline of the unfinished long edge and a second row ¼" (6mm) from the first, on the seam allowance (B). The two rows of gathering stitches help control and direct the fullness. In addition, the second row acts as your safety net—if a thread breaks on one row, you can still gather without having to restitch. For additional information on machine gathering, refer to Gathering, pages 103–5.*

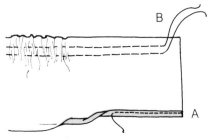

3. *With right sides together, pin the ruffle strip to the garment,*

matching ends, seams and marking points.

4. *To gather, secure one end of the gathering threads by wrapping them in a figure eight around a pin. Working from the other end, gently pull up on the bobbin threads, adjusting the gathers until they are evenly distributed. Secure the gathering threads. Pin baste or hand baste the ruffle in place, then machine stitch it along the seamline, just below the row of gathering stitches (C).*

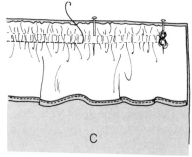

5. *Trim the seam allowances to ⅜" (10mm). Press the seam allowances flat, then toward the garment. If you wish, you can hold the seam allowances securely in place by edgestitching the seam on the garment through all the layers (D).*

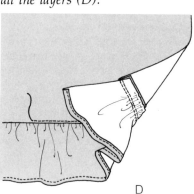

Double This type of ruffle is made from a wide strip of fabric folded in half lengthwise which automatically finishes one edge, eliminating the hem.

1. *With right sides together, stitch the short ends to form a circle. Press the seam allowances open. With wrong sides together, fold the fabric in half, raw edges meeting, and press.*

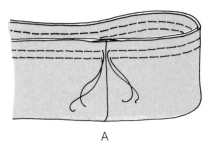

2. *To prepare (A), pin, gather and stitch (B) a double ruffle to a garment edge, follow steps 2 to 4 for the Single Ruffle, above.*

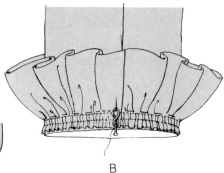

3. *Press the seam allowances flat (C), then toward the garment. As you press, avoid touching the ruffled area with your iron so you don't set in wrinkles or creases.*

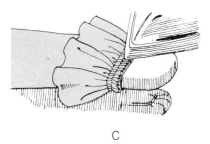

C

RUFFLES ENCLOSED IN A SEAM

Either single or double ruffles can be enclosed in a seam. Hem a single ruffle before you begin; fold a double ruffle in half lengthwise and press. See the relevant step 1 on page 152 to finish the ends. Prepare the ruffle for gathering, using two rows of long machine stitches.

1. *Pin the ruffle to the edge of one garment section, right sides together, matching ends, seams and marking points. Adjust the gathers, then smooth the ruffle to make sure that the body of the ruffle will not be caught in the permanent stitching.*

2. *Machine stitch the ruffle in place ⅛" (3mm) from the stitching line, on the seam allowance (A).*

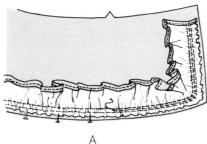

A

3. *With right sides together, pin the garment section with the ruffle to the other garment section. The ruffle is sandwiched between the right sides of both sections.*

4. *With the ruffled garment section on top, stitch along the seamline through all layers, next to the previous stitching, being careful not to catch the body of the ruffle in your stitching (B). Trim, grade and clip the edges and corners. Press the seam allowances flat, then turn the garment section to the outside. Finish the garment edge according to the pattern directions.*

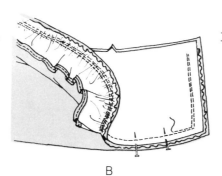

B

Here's a quick way to use your overlock machine to cut out and hem single ruffles. With a water soluble or air erasable marking pen, draw lines on your fabric to indicate the width of the ruffle, including a seam allowance for gathering. Guide the fabric through the overlock machine so that one edge of the ruffle is cut and finished in one step. If piecing is necessary, do it after the ruffle sections are cut and hemmed.

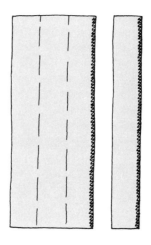

For more information:

see GATHERING.

on Edgestitching, see under MACHINE STITCHING.

see OVERLOCK STITCHING.

on Trimming, Grading and Clipping, see under SEAMS.

on Pressing, see under WHAT TO KNOW BEFORE YOU SEW.

Seams

The techniques for creating accurate seams are easy to learn. Get into the habit of making a test seam before you begin any new project. That way, before you actually sew on the garment, you'll know if any machine adjustments need to be made. Using the thread you intend to use, take two 12" (30.5cm)-long strips of your fashion fabric and stitch them together as if you were sewing a garment seam. Take a close look at the test seam to see if any adjustments need to be made:

▶ Is the sewing machine's tension or pressure correct? What changes need to be made?

▶ Is a different type or size of thread required?

▶ Is the sewing machine needle the proper size and free of defects?

▶ Does the fabric require extra pinning or basting to keep it from shifting as you sew?

Correcting any of these problems early in your sewing will save valuable time later.

STRAIGHT-STITCHED SEAMS

Straight-stitched seams, sometimes called plain seams, are made with one row of stitching. They are the basis for most other seams.

1. *Before basting the fabric sections together, determine the best direction for stitching the seam. Directional stitching prevents the seam areas from stretching as you stitch. Seams should be stitched in the direction of the grain, unless there are intersecting seams to be matched near one end of the seam. In that case, start stitching from the end with the intersections so you can match them easily. If you have difficulty recognizing the direction of the grain, run your finger along the cut edge of the seam allowance. If you're going with the grain, the threads along the edge should lay smooth; if you're going against the grain, the threads will come loose and the edge may begin to fray. Without testing, you can generally stitch from the widest to the narrowest part of each garment piece.*

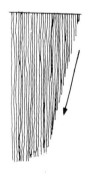

2. *Working with right sides together, baste the two layers of fabric together, matching notches and markings. For most fabrics, pin basting is enough to hold the layers firmly in place. Insert the pins at right angles to the fabric edge, keeping the pin heads on the seam allowance (A). This makes them easier to remove as you sew. Never, never stitch over the pins—it can break or damage your needle.*

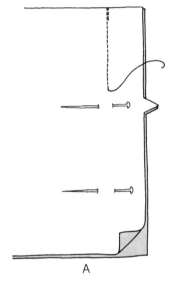

A

If pin basting is not sufficient, refer to the section on Basting, pages 52–54. If you choose double-faced basting tape, be sure to test it first on scraps of your garment fabric. The tape should hold the layers firmly in place and you should be able to remove it without damaging the surface of the fabric in any way. To be sure you don't stitch through the tape, making it difficult or impossible to remove, place it on the seam allowance, ¼" (6mm) away from the stitching line. Remove the tape before pressing (B).

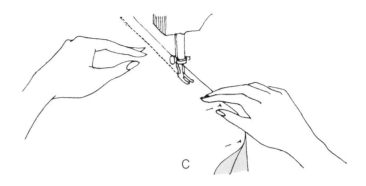

C

B

3. Place the garment sections to be seamed under the presser foot so that the seam allowances are to the right of the presser foot and the rest of the garment is to the left. Always check your pattern instructions for seam width before you sew. Although seam-lines are usually ⅝" (15mm) from the cut edge, they may be wider or narrower. Beginning ½" (13mm) from the top of the seam, lower the needle into the fabric so that it falls exactly on the seamline. Lower the presser foot and backstitch for ½" (13mm) until you reach the top of the seam, then stitch forward,

exactly *over the first stitches, and continue until you reach the end of the seam (C). To reinforce the end, backstitch for ½" (13mm), over the seam stitches.*

4. *To help you make sure seams stay uniform in width as you stitch, use a seam guide.*

▶ *Many machines come with a stitching guide etched into the throat plate (D). If you have cut the fabric out so the edge is smooth and you keep the edge of the fabric aligned with the proper marking, the seam width remains even as you sew.*

▶ *Some machines have an additional seam guide attachment that can be adjusted to different seam widths (E). This is especially useful for curved seams.*

▶ *If your machine does not have a stitching guide, create your own with a piece of masking tape or adhesive tape. Place it on the throat plate, to the right of the needle and parallel to the presser foot, so that the distance between the needle and one of the edges of the tape is the desired width (F).*

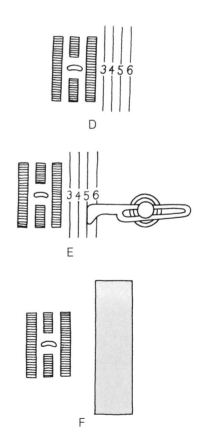

D

E

F

Pressing Seams All seams are pressed in the same two-step operation. First, press the seam flat along the stitching line to blend the stitches (G), then press it open (H). Certain seams, like the mock flat-fell seam, may require a third pressing step, such as pressing the seam allowances to one side, or special equipment such as brown paper strips. For more information, refer to the section on Pressing Equipment, pages 39–41.

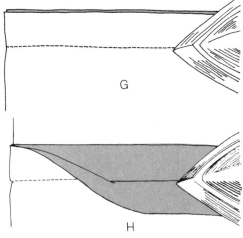

G

H

Knife-edged appliqué scissors with one large and one small blade make a great grading tool. The larger blade holds the layers of fabric so you can see exactly where you are cutting while both blades trim the fabric.

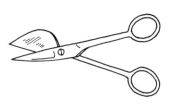

Trimming Seams Cutting the seam allowances to a narrower width reduces bulk. Seams are trimmed before the seam is pressed.

1. *Enclosed seam allowances, such as those in collars, cuffs, bands and facings, should be trimmed to ¼" (6mm).*

2. *Trim the corners diagonally at the end of a seam (I), particularly if it will cross another seam later on.*

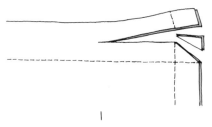

I

Grading Seams Trim *each* seam allowance to a different width so that no ridge forms on the outside of the garment if both seam allowances are turned in the same direction. Grading also helps seams lie flat without bulk (J). Leave the seam allowance that is closest to the garment the widest. Trim completely enclosed seams, such as those on collars, cuffs and bands, narrower than the more exposed seams enclosed in facings.

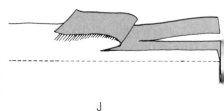

J

Corners Reinforce *inside corners,* such as those on a square neckline, or corners that need to be clipped for sewing, with an extra row of stitches before the seam is sewn (K). Depending on the pattern instructions, clip the corner before or after the seam is stitched.

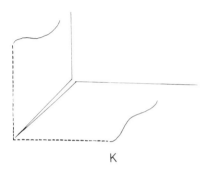

K

Reinforce *outside corners,* such as those on collars, as the seam is stitched.

1. *As you stitch the corner, shorten the stitch length to about 15 to 20 stitches per inch (per 2.5cm) on either side of the corner. When you reach the point, take one or two smaller stitches diagonally across it (L).*

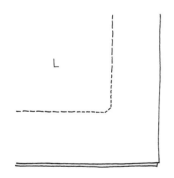

L

2. *Trim and grade the seam allowances, then trim off the corner point seam allowances close*

to the stitching. If the angle is 90 degrees or more, trim off the excess in one wedge (M). If the angle is less than 90 degrees, trim off the excess in three wedges (N).

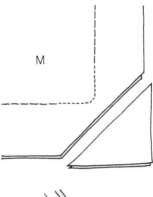

M

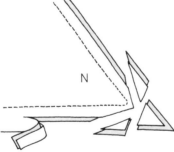

N

3. *After pressing the seam flat, press it open. A point presser will make it easier to get into the corners (O).*

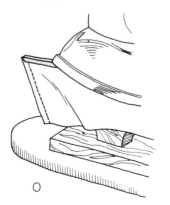

O

4. *Fold the seam allowances under on each side and press. Because the corners are already trimmed, they will meet at an angle to form a miter (P). Turn the garment section to the outside and press again.*

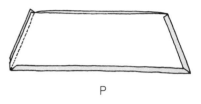

P

When turning a corner in an enclosed seam to the outside, don't use the tip of your scissors as a pushing tool—it's too easy to poke right through the stitches. Instead, do one of the following:

■ Use a point turner, a notion with a narrow, slightly blunted tip, to push out the corner.

■ Before stitching the corner, place a length of knotted thread between the layers exactly at the corner. Position the thread so that the knot is on the seam allowance. Stitch over the thread as you sew the seam. When you trim the corner, be careful not to cut off the knot. Once the garment section is turned, use the thread ends to pull the corner points out; then remove the threads.

Curves To make curves lie flat, they must be notched or clipped. The seams must be trimmed and graded, pressed flat, then notched or clipped before they are pressed open.

When you clip or notch, be careful to cut just to, but not through, the stitching line. Your pattern instructions may recommend staystitching a curved area before the seam is sewn. If so, clip or notch just to the line of staystitching.

The number and distance between each clip or notch depends on the sharpness of the curve. As a general rule, space clips or notches approximately ½" to 1" (13mm to 2.5cm) apart. Deep curves require more clips or notches than gradual curves.

On *inside curves*, clip by taking small *snips* into the seam allowance just to the line of stitching (A).

On *outside curves*, cut small *wedges*, or *notches*, from the seam allowance (B).

If you are joining an outside curve to an inside curve, such as on a princess seam, one seam allowance must be notched and the other clipped after stay-stitching if the seams are to lie flat when pressed open.

TOPSTITCHED SEAMS

The topstitched seam is a straight-stitched seam with a decorative treatment. Extra rows of stitching are done on the right side of the fabric immediately after the basic seam is completed, while the garment section is still easy to handle.

Because the topstitched seam is often used to highlight the design features of a garment, it is most effective on solid or lightly textured or printed fabrics. Use a matching or contrasting color thread. Or, to give your topstitching more definition, try using topstitching thread. Because it has a slightly thicker ply than all-purpose thread, it will give the topstitching a more prominent appearance, particularly useful on heavier fabrics such as denim and corduroy. Topstitching thread can be used in both the top and the bobbin of the machine, or just on the top with all-purpose thread in the bobbin.

A *single-topstitched seam*, as a purely decorative or finishing technique for garment edges, has one row of stitching that runs parallel to the seamline.

1. *After stitching and pressing the seam, press both seam allowances to the side you plan to topstitch.*

2. *Working on the right side of the garment section, add a row of topstitching parallel to and ¼" (6mm) away from the seamline (C).*

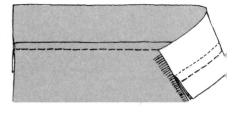

C

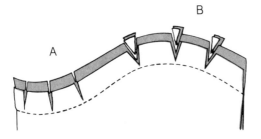

B

A

If you're having trouble keeping your stitching straight, practice the eyeballing technique. Don't watch the needle as you sew. Instead, keep your eyes on the edge of the fabric, making sure it is aligned with the proper marking on the throat plate.

Double-topstitched seams are ideal if the fabric is particularly thick and hard to press; this technique helps keep the seam allowances flat.

1. *Make a straight-stitched seam and press the seam allowances open.*

2. *Working on the right side of the garment section, topstitch either 1/8" (3mm) or 1/4" (6mm) away from, and on either side of, the seamline. Keep the topstitching parallel to the seamline and make sure you topstitch through both the garment and the seam allowance (A).*

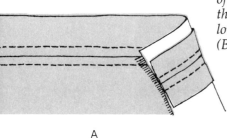

A

MOCK FLAT-FELL SEAM

This is an easy way to create the look of the more intricately constructed flat-fell seam. The three rows of stitching make a very secure seam treatment that can withstand a lot of rough-and-tumble play.

1. *With right sides together, make a straight-stitched seam. Press the seam allowances open, then press them to one side.*

2. *Working on the outside of the garment section, edgestitch next to the seam, then topstitch 1/4" (6mm) from the seam, through the seam allowances. Both rows of stitching should be parallel to the seamline. Trim the seam allowances close to the stitching (B).*

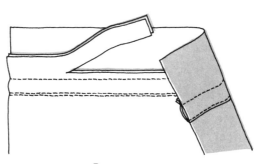

B

When topstitching on a looped or nubby fabric, try stitching with a medium-length, narrow zigzag stitch. The zigzag stitch blends in with the nubby texture and does not flatten the loops as much as a straight stitch would.

OVERLOCK SEAMS

Seams sewn on the overlock machine call for a different set of techniques than those sewn on conventional sewing machines. If you own an overlock machine, mastering these methods can increase your sewing pleasure and efficiency. Refer to the section on Overlock Stitching, pages 129–36, for more information.

For more information:

on Basting Tape and Pin Basting, see under BASTING.

on Backstitching, Reinforcement Stitching and Staystitching, see under MACHINE STITCHING.

on Edgestitching, Topstitching and Zigzag Stitching, see under MACHINE STITCHING.

see OVERLOCK STITCHING.

Seam Finishes

Proper seam finishes can make a child's garment last longer as the more durable seams can stand up to repeated washing and wearing. In addition, young skin may be sensitive to scratchy or unfinished surfaces, so seam finishes are an important comfort factor in children's clothes.

STITCHED AND PINKED

This finish is a good choice for fabrics that don't ravel easily and for heavyweight fabrics because it does not add bulk.

After the seam is stitched and pressed open, stitch along the length of each seam allowance, ¼" (6mm) from the raw edge. Using pinking shears, trim the raw edge of each seam allowance.

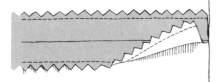

TURNED AND STITCHED

This finish is sometimes referred to as a *clean finish*. Use it to provide a neat, tailored appearance on light- and medium-weight fabrics. It's also a good choice for unlined jackets, provided the fabric is not too bulky.

1. *Make a straight-stitched seam, pressing the seam allowances open. Turn the raw edge of each seam allowance under ¼" (6mm) and press, if necessary.*

2. *Folding the garment section out of the way, edgestitch close to the folded edge of each seam allowance.*

3. *If your fabric is hard to handle, making it difficult to fold and stitch the raw edges, here's a way to control the edges. Before turning the raw edge under, fold the garment section out of the way and machine stitch along the length of each seam allowance, ¼" (6mm) from the raw edge. Fold the seam allowance under along this stitching line and, at the same time, edgestitch close to the foldline.*

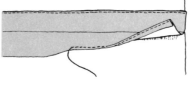

MACHINE ZIGZAG

The machine zigzag finish is a quick and easy finishing technique for fabrics that tend to ravel easily. Using this procedure, you can finish the edges of the garment before any seams are sewn, while the sections are still flat, or you can finish each seam as it is stitched.

Pretest this finish on a scrap of your fashion fabric to determine the best stitch length and width. Narrower stitches are generally best for lightweight fabrics and wider ones for bulkier fabrics. Once you have de-termined the best stitch length and width, stitch close to the raw edge of the fabric. On the right-hand swing of the zigzag, the needle should go over the edge of the fabric.

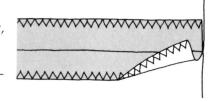

OVERLOCK FINISH

Many conventional sewing machines have a special overcast, or overedge, finishing stitch. The stitch made by an overlock machine is also a finishing stitch. Any of these stitches are appropriate finishing techniques for a straight-stitched seam.

Regardless of the type of overcast or overlock stitch, the decision to finish the edges before or after the seam is sewn is entirely up to you. When you are working on the small detail areas common to children's clothing, or if you are sewing for speed, you may find it easier to finish the edges before the garment sections are sewn together.

BOUND FINISHES

The applied seam finish, also called a *bound seam,* provides a neat, professional look to seams that may be visible, such as those in an unlined jacket or coat, or for fabrics that ravel easily. The edges of each seam allowance are encased in strips of bias material, such as double-fold bias tape, or strips of sheer tricot, such as Seams Great® or Seam Saver™.

Bias Double-fold bias tape comes in different colors which can be used to finish and conceal raw edges very attractively.

1. *With right sides together, make a straight-stitched seam and press the seam allowances open.*

2. *Cut two strips of double-fold bias tape equal to the length of the seam edges to be bound. If you are binding curved seams, preshape the binding. (Preshaping, on page 60, tells you how to do this.) Encase one raw edge in the tape, placing the wider side of the tape underneath and the narrower side on the top. To hold the tape in place for stitching, use pins inserted at right angles to the seam edge.*

3. *Working with the narrow side of the tape facing up, edgestitch close to the inner fold of the tape, stitching through the seam allowance and both layers of the tape. Repeat the procedure for the other seam allowance.*

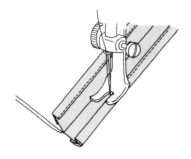

Tricot This binding material, available in ⅝" (15mm) and 1¼" (3.2cm) widths, provides a very lightweight, nonbulky finish. Because it is extremely flexible, it's particularly useful on curved seams.

1. *With right sides together, make a straight-stitched seam and press the seam allowances open.*

2. *Tricot bindings are not prefolded but they do have built-in "curl." To determine which way to apply the binding, stretch it gently and observe the direction of the curl. The binding should be applied so that it curls around the raw edge of the fabric.*

To apply the binding, use either a straight or a zigzag stitch. Beginning at the top of one seam allowance, fold the binding around the raw edge of the fabric and anchor it with a pin. Take one or two stitches

near the edge of the binding, remove the pin, and continue to stitch, stretching the binding gently as you go, allowing it to curl over the raw edge. Repeat the procedure for the other seam allowance.

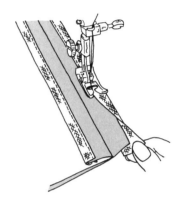

A liquid seam sealant, such as Fray Check, is particularly useful as a seam finish for small detail areas. Protect your garment from accidental drips of sealant by putting paper toweling between the garment and the seam allowance. Apply a thin bead of sealant along each cut edge.

For more information:

on Double-fold Bias Tape, see under BINDINGS.

on Edgestitching and Zigzag Stitching, see under MACHINE STITCHING.

see OVERLOCK STITCHING.

Sleeves and Sleeve Finishes

Children are happiest when their clothes fit well, are comfortable and can withstand the strain of active play. Well-constructed sleeves are an important part of this formula.

There are three basic types of sleeves.

▶ A **set-in sleeve** is attached to the garment at the shoulder in a seam that encircles the arm. The top of the sleeve, called the sleeve cap, may include fullness that needs to be eased, gathered or pleated to make the sleeve fit into the armhole opening of the garment. Any garment designed so that the armhole seam is lower than the natural shoulder line has a dropped or extended shoulder. It's a very comfortable style with a flat sleeve cap, and a popular, easy-to-construct style for children's clothing, particularly play clothes.

▶ A **raglan sleeve** may be identified by seams that extend diagonally from the neckline area to the underarm.

▶ A **kimono sleeve** is cut as part of the bodice or yoke front and back. It is joined together by a shoulder seam and an underarm seam.

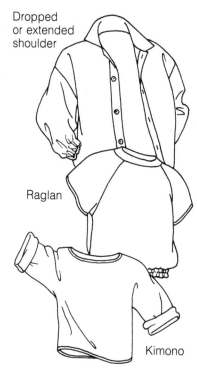

Dropped or extended shoulder

Raglan

Kimono

Set-in sleeve

THE FLAT CONSTRUCTION METHOD

It's easy to construct sleeves by this method:

1. Unless you are making a raglan sleeve, stitch the garment together at the shoulders, but leave the side seams open.

2. If your sleeve has a finishing detail such as a dart opening, finish it before doing anything else on the sleeve.

3. Finish the lower edge of the sleeve. Depending on the style of the sleeve, this may include finishing and attaching a cuff, applying binding or elastic or hemming the lower edge.

4. If the sleeve cap requires any special treatment, such as ease-stitching, gathering or pleating, do this as your next step.

5. Sew the sleeve to the garment from underarm to underarm.

6. Sew the garment together at sides and underarms in one continuous seam.

SET-IN SLEEVES

Before you begin, stitch the garment together at the shoulders and the side seams, creating the armhole.

1. *For a sleeve cap with fullness, consult your pattern instructions, then gather or ease-stitch the sleeve cap between the symbols, using two rows of gathering stitches.*

2. *Stitch the sleeve underarm seam. Finish the lower edge of your sleeve according to your pattern instructions or using the hemming method most suitable for your fabric.*

3. *Working with the garment wrong side out, place the sleeve in the armhole, right sides together. Pin the sleeve and the garment together along the armhole seamline, matching underarm seams and symbols (A).*

4. *Pull up the easing or gathering threads until the sleeve fits the armhole. On an eased sleeve, the straight grain that occurs at the top of the sleeve cap does not permit easing. Therefore, leave about 1" (2.5cm) of the sleeve cap flat and uneased at the shoulder seam. Secure the thread ends around a pin in a figure eight (B).*

5. *Check to be sure the easing or the gathering is evenly distributed, then hand baste the sleeve in place along the seamline (C).*

6. *With the sleeve side facing you, machine stitch along the seamline, beginning at the underarm (D). For additional security, stitch again ¼" (6mm)*

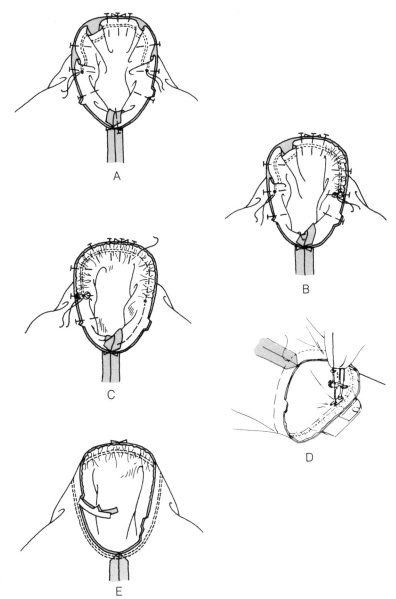

A

B

C

D

E

away, on the seam allowance. To reduce bulk, trim the seam allowance close to this second row of stitching (E). If the garment is unlined, overcast or zigzag the seam allowances to prevent raveling.

7. *Working over a tailor's ham or a press mitt, press the seam flat, then toward the sleeve using the tip of your iron. Avoid the sleeve cap area so you don't press in unnecessary creases.*

163

RAGLAN SLEEVE

For the raglan sleeve, the front and back of the garment are stitched together after the sleeve is inserted.

1. Finish the lower edge of the sleeve according to the pattern instructions or use the hemming method most suitable for your fabric (A).

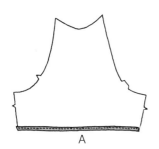

A

2. With right sides together, pin the long, curved edges of the sleeve to the garment front and back, matching notches and other symbols. Stitch along the seamlines. Trim and clip the seam allowance between the notches and the underarm (B).

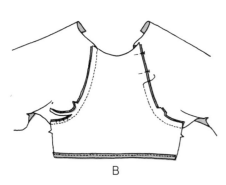

B

3. Press the seams open; then pin the side seams together and stitch from the lower edge of the sleeve to the lower edge of the garment in one continuous line of stitching (C). Clip at the angle formed under the arm and press the seam open.

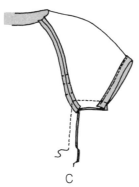

C

KIMONO SLEEVES

Before you begin, stitch the garment front and garment back sections together at the shoulder seam and press the seam open.

1. Finish the lower edge of the sleeve according to your pattern instructions or use the hemming method most suitable for your fabric.

2. Pin the garment front to the garment back along the underarm seam and stitch together from the lower edge of the garment to the lower edge of the sleeve in one continuous line of stitching.

3. To keep the underarm area from ripping out, add a second row of short stitches, approximately 15 to 20 stitches per inch (per 2.5cm), at the underarm

curve, on the seam allowance (A).

4. Clip just to, but not through, the reinforcement stitches in the underarm area (B). Press the seam open over a press mitt or tailor's ham.

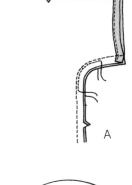

A

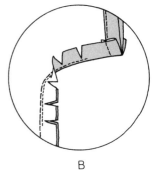

B

Do you get confused trying to remember which is the front and which is the back of a sleeve or bodice? One notch at the armhole area indicates the front; two notches indicates the back.

SLEEVE FINISHES

When a sleeve becomes very narrow at the lower edge, some type of opening is usually required for the child's hand. Three types occur on children's clothes—dart, seam and hemmed openings.

Dart Opening This is usually accompanied by a cuff or a band. It works best on lightweight fabrics. Construct the dart opening first, while the sleeve is still flat.

1. *Stitch the dart along the lines indicated, then slash the dart to the point shown by the pattern marking (A).*

2. *Fold the raw edges of the opening to the wrong side of the garment and press them flat (B).*

3. *Turn the raw edges under to finish them and edgestitch or slipstitch them to the garment (C).*

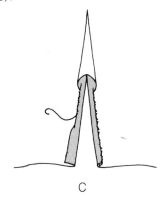

C

Seam Opening This is one of the easiest sleeve finishes. It is usually constructed as part of the sleeve underarm seam. This technique works best on lightweight to mediumweight fabrics.

1. *Stitch the sleeve seam, ending the stitching where indicated by the pattern markings. Backstitch to secure (A). Press the seam open above the pattern marking.*

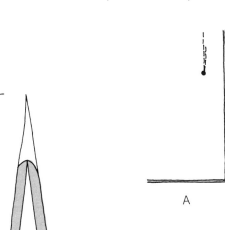

A

B

A

For added security on a dart opening, finish the raw edge at the top of the slash with Fray Check.

165

2. *Turn the raw edges of the opening to the wrong side of the sleeve along the foldline and press (B).*

3. *Turn the raw edges of the opening under again to meet the crease (C), tapering to nothing above the pattern symbol. Press again.*

B   C

4. *Edgestitch along the sides and across the top of the opening (D).*

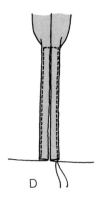

D

Narrow Hem Opening This is a common fast sleeve finish on blouses and dresses made in lightweight fabrics.

1. *Reinforce the lower edge of the sleeve by stitching along the seamline as indicated by the pattern markings. Extend the reinforcement stitching approximately ½" (13mm) beyond each pattern marking. Clip to, but not through, the stitching at each marking (A).*

2. *Narrow hem the seam allowance between the clips (B).*

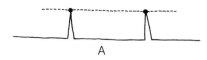

A

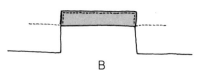

B

When constructing a narrow hem opening in a fabric that has a tendency to ravel, try sealing the edges of the clips with a liquid seam sealant, such as Fray Check. Test this first on a scrap of the fashion fabric to make sure no shading occurs.

For more information:

see DARTS.

see GATHERING.

on Slipstitching, see under HAND SEWING.

on Hemming Techniques, see under HEMS.

on Easestitching, Edgestitching and Reinforcement Stitching, see under MACHINE STITCHING.

on Clipping and Trimming, see under SEAMS.

on Pressing Techniques and Equipment, see under WHAT TO KNOW BEFORE YOU SEW.

Smocking

A centuries-old art with a delicate, decorative appearance, smocking is basically a series of pleats held together by rows of special continuous embroidery stitches. Smocking controls fullness on dresses, pinafores and bonnets. When smocking is used as a trimming detail, a length of fabric is smocked, then applied as an insertion to the main garment sections.

ADDING A SMOCKED INSERT

Children's patterns that have smocking detail already include the fullness necessary to create the pleats. However, to add a smocked insert on a garment that does not include it, the general rule is that 3" (7.5cm) of flat fabric is required for every inch (2.5cm) of finished smocking.

1. Determine the length and width of the finished insert.

2. Cut a piece of fabric equal in width to the finished insert, plus two seam allowances, and equal in length to three times the finished insert, plus two seam allowances.

FABRICS AND NOTIONS

Any fabric that is lightweight enough to gather easily is suitable for smocking. Your choices include batiste, gingham, chambray, challis, broadcloth, crepe de chine, dotted swiss, muslin and percale.

The most commonly recommended thread for smocking is six-strand embroidery floss, since it can be separated into any required number of strands. Two or three strands are generally used, depending on the fineness of the fabric. The best needle to use is a #7 or #8 crewel needle. For more information on needles and thread, refer to the section on Hand Embroidery, pages 84–85.

MARKING

Professional results begin with accurate marking, since rows of evenly spaced dots are the guidelines for the stitches and the pleats.

There are two basic smocking techniques: regular and English.

▶ *In **regular smocking,** the dots are marked on the right side of the fabric. Then the embroidery stitches are worked from dot to dot so that the pleats are created as the stitches are formed.*

▶ *In **English smocking,** the dots are marked on the wrong side of the fabric. A running stitch is used to connect the dots and draw the fabric up into evenly spaced pleats. Then rows of embroidery stitches are applied to the surface of the fabric so that the pleats are permanently secured and the embroidery stitches are not visible on the wrong side of the fabric. Once the embroidery is completed, the running stitches are removed.*

The finished appearance of the smocking is the same, regardless of which method is used. However, because it is easier to use a combination of stitches with the English method, it is the most common method and the one used in this book.

To achieve even-looking smocking with a professional appearance, it is essential that the dots be evenly spaced and in parallel rows. The easiest way to accomplish this is with a sheet of transfer dots. If your pattern includes smocking as a design feature, transfer dots are provided. If you are designing your own smocking detail, transfer sheets of dots may be purchased in many needlework and fabric stores.

When transferring the dots to your fabric, follow the manufacturer's directions carefully, making a test sample first. If the ink smears or the dots are not removable, either choose another fabric or transfer the dots onto the *wrong* side of your fabric, using dressmaker's tracing paper and a pencil.

Make sure that you transfer the dots so that the rows are parallel to the lengthwise and crosswise grain of the fabric. This guarantees that the finished smocking will fall into even, graceful folds.

PREGATHERING

To pregather, use two continuous strands of contrasting thread, or one strand of heavy-duty thread, for each row of running stitches. Once the pleats are completed, the sewing lines

form a guide for the rows of embroidery stitches. When the embroidery stitches are completed, remove the running stitches.

Because it cannot be joined in the middle, the thread must be long enough to complete the row of stitches. Knot the end of the thread before you begin.

1. *Working on the* wrong *side of the fabric and starting at the end of one horizontal row of dots, insert the needle into the fabric at one side of the first dot and bring it out at the other side so that you are picking up just a few threads of the fabric. Work across the entire row, picking up each succeeding dot so that long running stitches form between the dots. Repeat for the remaining horizontal rows of dots. Leave long thread tails (A).*

2. *Pull up on all the threads at one time, forming straight, close, even pleats, until the fabric section is equal to the size indicated in your pattern instructions or to the desired finished size plus seam allowances. Knot each set of threads securely (B).*

3. *Place the fabric on a flat surface and smooth the pleats so that the pleats are evenly spaced. Hold the iron slightly above the fabric and steam, never resting the iron on the fabric (C). Let the pleated fabric dry thoroughly before doing the decorative stitches.*

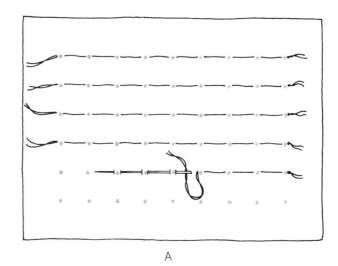

A

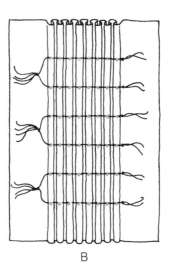

B

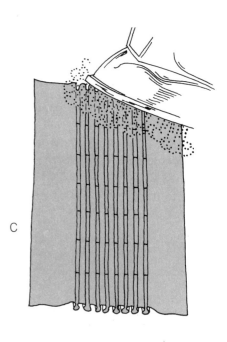

C

STITCHES

Beautiful smocking designs are created by combining and arranging the stitches to form different patterns. Use three strands of embroidery floss for all stitches. Be careful that you do not pull the smocking stitches too tight—the finished work should have some give. As you sew, catch only a few threads at the top of each pleat.

Cable Stitch Use one row of running stitches as a guide. A line of stitches alternating above and below the running stitches creates the cable pattern.

1. *Working from left to right, bring the needle up through the fabric on row A at the left side of pleat 1, slightly above one row of running stitches. With the floss above the needle, take a stitch through pleat 2 so that the needle emerges slightly below the row of running stitches.*

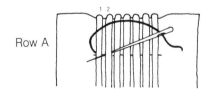

2. *Pull the needle down so that the floss forms a tight stitch. Holding the floss below the needle, take a stitch through*

pleat 3 so that the needle emerges slightly above the row of running stitches.

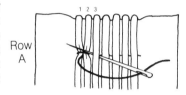

3. *Pull the needle up so that the floss forms a tight stitch. Continue across the fabric, alternating the stitches in the same manner.*

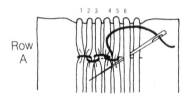

Diamond Stitch Use three rows of running stitches as guidelines for the two rows of embroidery stitches that create the diamond pattern.

1. *Working from left to right, bring the needle up through the fabric on row A at the left side of pleat 1. With the floss above the needle, take a stitch through pleat 2.*

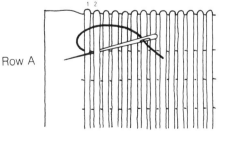

2. *Draw up the floss to form a tight stitch. Keeping the floss above the needle, drop down to row B and take a stitch through pleat 3.*

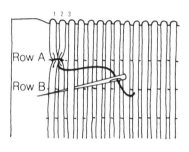

3. *Working with the floss below the needle, and continuing on row B, take a stitch through pleat 4 and draw up the floss.*

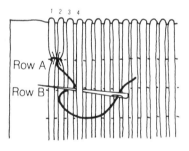

4. *Return to row A, and, keeping the floss below the needle, take a stitch through pleat 5.*

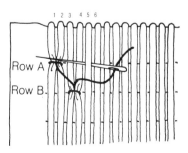

5. *With the floss* above *the needle, take a stitch in pleat 6 and draw up the floss.*

6. *Continue across the two rows, alternating the stitches in the same manner.*

7. *Beginning at pleat 1 on row C, repeat the stitches, working back and forth between row C and row B to complete the diamond pattern. As you sew, reverse the position of the floss in relation to the needle so that the stitches above and below each other form a mirror image. Two sets of stitches will form along row B.*

Feather Stitch This stitch creates a gradual zigzag pattern between three rows of running stitches. To make each stitch, hold the floss to the left and *underneath* the needle, forming a loop.

1. *Bring the needle through the fabric on row A at the right side of pleat 1. Working from right to left, insert the needle through the top of pleat 1.*

2. *Draw up the floss. Insert the needle into pleat 2, slightly below the first stitch.*

3. *Draw up the floss. Repeat, tapering the stitches down to pleat 6, row C. Repeat again, tapering the stitches up to pleat 11, row A. Continue across the fabric in the same manner.*

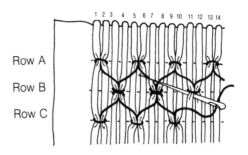

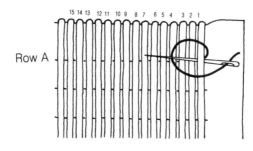

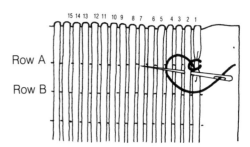

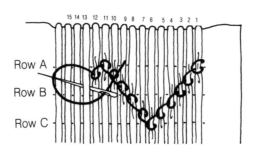

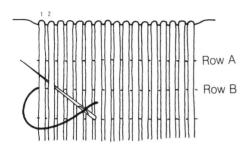

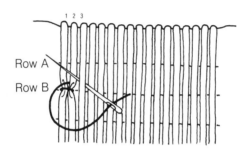

Row A

Row B

Row A

Row B

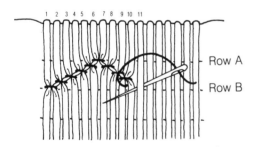

Row A

Row B

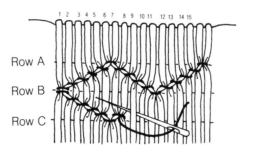

Row A

Row B

Row C

Narrow Trellis Stitch This stitch creates a latticework pattern. As you taper the stitches up, keep the floss *below* the needle; as you taper the stitches down, keep the floss *above* the needle.

1. *Bring the needle through the fabric on row B at the left side of pleat 1.*

2. *Keeping the floss* below *the needle, insert the needle from right to left into pleat 2.*

3. *Draw up the floss. Repeat, inserting the needle into pleat 3, slightly above the first stitch. Repeat, tapering the stitches up to pleat 6, row A.*

4. *Working with the floss* above *the needle, repeat, tapering the stitches down to pleat 11, row B.*

5. *Continue across the fabric, repeating steps 2 to 4.*

6. *Repeat the trellis stitch again across the fabric. This time, begin at pleat 1, row B, and taper down to pleat 6, row C. Taper up to pleat 11, row B. Continue across the fabric in the same manner.*

Van Dyke Stitch Use two rows of running stitches as guidelines to create this stitch that joins alternate pleats together in a tight zigzag pattern.

1. *Working from right to left, bring the needle through the fabric on row A at the right side of pleat 1, then insert it through the tops of pleats 1 and 2.*

2. *With the floss above the needle, insert the needle back through the same two pleats.*

3. *Draw up the floss. Bring the needle down to row B and insert it through the tops of pleats 2 and 3. Working with the floss below the needle, insert the needle back through the same two pleats.*

4. *Draw up the floss. Continue across the two rows in the same manner. As you sew, reverse the position of the floss in relation to the needle so that the stitches above and below each other form a mirror image.*

Wide Trellis Stitch This stitch is similar to the narrow trellis but it is worked in a wider pattern across six rows of running stitches rather than three.

1. *Bring the needle up through the fabric at the left side of pleat 1, between rows C and D.*

2. *Keeping the floss below the needle, insert the needle from right to left into pleat 2.*

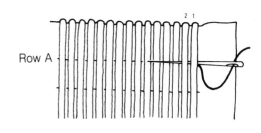

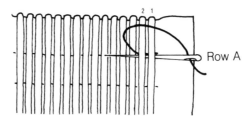

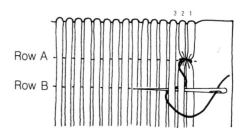

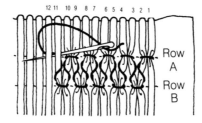

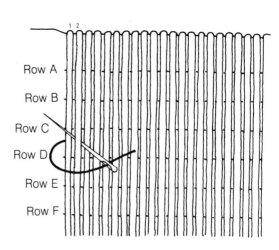

172

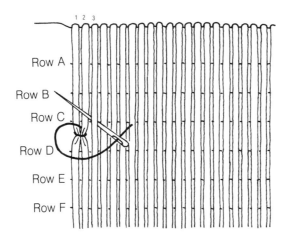

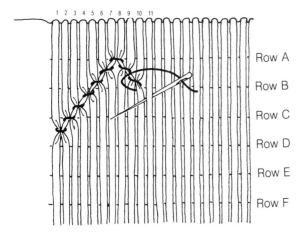

3. *Draw up the floss. Repeat, inserting the needle into pleat 3, slightly above the first stitch.*

4. *Draw up the floss. Repeat, tapering the stitches up to pleat 7, row A. Working with the floss* above *the needle, repeat, tapering the stitches down to pleat 13, between rows C and D.*

5. *Continue across the fabric, repeating steps 2 to 4.*

6. *Repeat the trellis stitch again across the fabric. This time, begin at pleat 1, between rows C and D, and taper down to pleat 7, row F, then taper up to pleat 13, between rows C and D.*

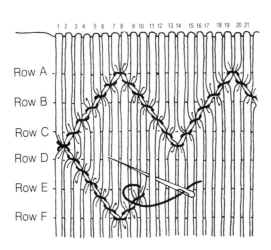

ACCENT STITCHES

These stitches add the finishing touch to a smocking design. Because they are sewn on the surface of the fabric, they can be applied before or after the running stitches are removed.

Lazy Daisy Stitch Use a series of lazy daisy stitches radiating from a center point to create a flower. Use a single stitch to create a leaf.

1. *Bring the needle up through the fabric between pleats 1 and 2.*

2. *Working from right to left and holding the floss above and to the left of the needle, insert the needle a thread or two from the first insertion. Bring the needle up between pleats 3 and 4, and draw up the floss to form a loop.*

3. *To secure the loop, insert the needle between pleats 3 and 4, to the left of the loop, and pull the floss to the wrong side of the fabric.*

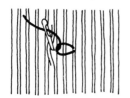

Rosebud Stitch A French knot with several straight stitches around it creates a rosebud effect.

1. *To form the French knot, bring the needle up through the fabric where you want the knot to be. Holding the floss taut in your left hand, wind it twice around the needle while you hold the needle almost flat against the fabric (A). Insert the needle back into the fabric a thread or two away from the first insertion (B) and gently pull the needle and thread through to form the knot (C).*

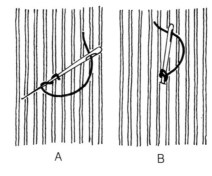

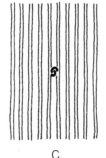

2. *For the straight stitches around the French knot, bring the needle up through the fabric next to the knot. Insert the needle next to the knot near the first insertion, then bring the needle back up a few threads away (D). Continue making straight stitches all around the knot (E).*

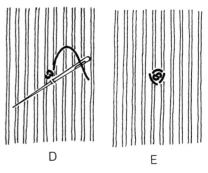

For more information:

on Running Stitches and Securing the Thread Ends, see under HAND SEWING.

on Dressmaker's Tracing Paper, see under WHAT TO KNOW BEFORE YOU SEW.

Snaps

Snaps are a practical fastener for overlapping garment edges that receive a minimum of strain, such as cuffs or neckline openings. Although they have less holding power than a hook and eye, snaps tend to be less bulky. Snaps can be the only fastener used to close a garment or they can serve as a back-up fastener, securing areas such as the corner of a neckline facing or a button closing.

Snaps are available in a variety of styles from sew-in types to multiple ones on a woven tape to no-sew gripper snaps that are attached with a hammer or a special tool. Snaps range in size from fine (4/0) to heavy (4). Regardless of the style, every snap has the same basic, two-part design: a ball half with an extension in the center, sewn on the underside of the overlap, and a socket half with an indented center to receive the ball, sewn on the upper layer of the garment section closest to the body.

SEW-ON SNAPS

These snaps are available in metal, with a black or nickel finish, and in clear nylon. Select the one that blends best with your fabric.

1. *Position the ball half of the snap on the underside of the overlap. Attach it to the garment by taking several small stitches close together through each hole. To keep the stitches from showing on the outside of the garment, pick up a thread of the*

fabric with each stitch and, as you work from hole to hole, tunnel the needle between the layers of fabric.

2. *To mark the location of the socket, rub the ball with tailor's chalk, then position the garment as it will be fastened so that the chalk marking is transferred to the underlap. Center the socket over the marking and sew it in place.*

GRIPPER SNAPS

These snaps require no sewing and are a strong, durable fastener—great for children's clothing. The ball and the socket halves each have a separate prong section. The socket prong may be a plain metal ring or decorated to look like a button.

The ring or decorated portion of the socket is positioned on the outside of the garment. The prongs go through to the wrong side of the fabric and hook into the socket. The stud is positioned on the right side of the underlap. The prongs come up from the wrong side of the fabric and hook into the stud.

These snaps come in different sizes. Choose the size according to the weight of your fabric. If the snap is too heavy, it will pull right through fabric that isn't strong enough to support it. If you need extra support, add one or two layers of interfacing between the garment and the seam allowance or facing.

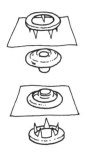

Most gripper snaps require a special tool for attaching them. A few manufacturers include attachment directions that use an eraser-tipped pencil, a hammer and a sturdy spool. No matter which method is used, the object is to press the prong and the snap section together to join them and securely attach them to the fabric.

Position gripper snaps the same way as sew-on snaps. Attach the ball half first, on the underside of the overlap, far enough from the edge so it will not show. Attach the socket half on the underlap so that it aligns with the ball.

SNAP TAPE

This is a casual fastener that looks best on children's play clothes and infants' wear. The snaps are preattached to a strip of woven tape. Because it's easy to apply, snap tape is a particularly good choice when a long row of snaps is required, such as at the inner leg seam on infants' wear. Once the tape is applied, the machine stitching will be visible on the outside of the garment.

Snap tape is available with two types of snaps. Sturdy *gripper snaps* on tape are especially useful for rugged fabrics such as denim and corduroy. *Plastic snaps*, heat-set into the tape, create a lighter-weight fastener suitable for knits and lighter-weight fabrics.

Regardless of the snap type, apply the tape to the garment in the same way. The seam allowances or the amount of overlap on the garment must be wider than the tape so that the tape edge won't show on the outside of the garment.

1. *Position the socket section of the tape on the underlap. Edgestitch the tape to the garment, through all the layers.*

2. *Align and position the ball section of the tape on the underside or seam allowance of the overlap. Edgestitch the tape to the overlap, through all the layers, using a zipper foot.*

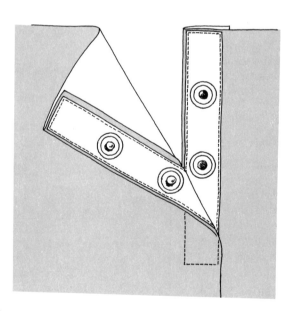

Trims

Sewing children's clothing presents a great opportunity to explore the fanciful world of ribbon, lace, picot edging, rickrack, piping, middy braid and bias tapes. The vast selection of styles and colors provides a stimulating, creative challenge that is part of the fun when you sew for kids.

Trim can be an integral part of the construction of the garment, such as bias binding that both finishes and decorates a raw edge. Or they can be purely decorative, to be added or not, as the child prefers. In fact, children's clothes offer you the chance to use the bits and pieces of trim left over from your larger projects.

When selecting your trims, there are a few things to keep in mind:

▶ *Choose trims with the same care requirements as the garment fabric.*

▶ *Avoid trims with rough or scratchy surfaces that can irritate a child's sensitive skin.*

▶ *Bypass trims with raised or looped surfaces that could easily be caught or pulled during active play, as well as trims with beading or tassels that could come loose and find their way into a little one's mouth.*

▶ *If you are adding trim to a pattern that does not include it as a design feature, you must figure the amount of the yardage for the trim yourself. Measure the garment area(s) to be trimmed, then purchase ½ yard (.5m) extra to allow for curves, corners and finishing the ends.*

APPLYING TRIMS

Trims can be sewn to almost any internal area of the garment, along an edge or inserted into a seam.

No matter which method you choose, for easy application, plan ahead so that you can apply the trim flat, before the final garment seam is sewn.

▶ *When using either the flat or the edging method, stitch all the garment seams except one, usually the center back seam. Apply the trim, then stitch the final seam.*

▶ *To insert the trim in a seam, apply it to one section of the garment before stitching the seam.*

Before machine stitching the trim to the garment, make a test sample to determine if any tension adjustments are necessary. If the stitches are too tight, the fabric underneath the trim, or even the trim itself, may pucker.

The Flat Method Use this method to apply any trim that is finished along both edges, such as rickrack, braid, ribbon and bands of lace.

Position trims accurately on the garment. If you are using a pattern that includes trim, transfer the placement lines from the pattern tissue to your fabric. To add trim to a pattern, decide where you want the trim to be, then mark the placement lines. Use the marking method suitable for your fabric.

1. Pin the trim along the placement lines. If the ends are not going to be caught in a seam, finish them after the trim is accurately positioned by turning them under ¼" (6mm) and pressing or pinning them in place (A).

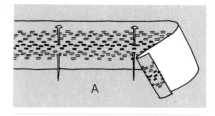

To apply a trim to a curved area, preshape it to match the garment curve by steam pressing, if the trim can withstand it. Be sure that you match the trim curve to the seamline, not the cutting line, since they may have different curves.

If you are applying trim to an extremely curved area, your best choice is a bias or knit trim.

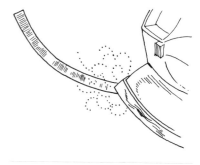

2. *If the trim is one that will not slip or ripple as you stitch, pin basting is sufficient. Otherwise, use a glue stick, disappearing basting tape, hand basting or fuse basting to hold the trim in place. To fuse baste, cut a strip of fusible web slightly narrower than the trim and, using steam and a press cloth, apply just enough heat and moisture to temporarily attach the trim to the garment.*

3. *Stitch the trim to the garment. When you are applying narrow trims or rickrack, stitch down the center (B). When you are applying wider flat trims, edgestitch along both sides (C).*

At a Corner: Miter the trim at a square corner for a flat, neat appearance.

1. *Edgestitch the trim to the garment along the outside edge, just to the point of the corner (D). Stop with the needle in the fabric and lift the presser foot. Pivot the trim and fabric, lower the presser foot and continue stitching along the edge (E).*

2. *Tuck the excess trim in at the corner to form a diagonal fold and pin it in place. Edgestitch along the inner edge of the trim (F). Finish the miter by hand sewing or machine stitching along the diagonal fold.*

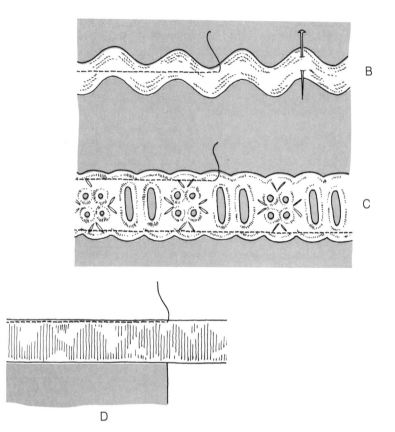

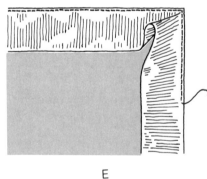

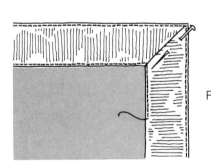

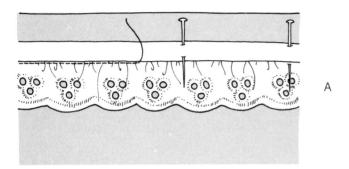

A

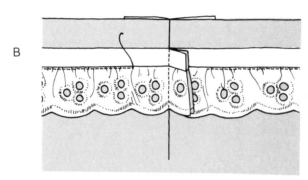

B

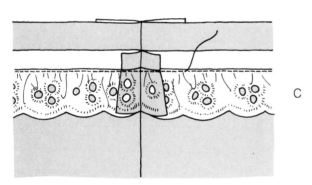

C

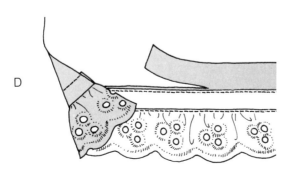

D

The Edging Method Some trims, such as piping, cording and fringes, as well as many laces and eyelets, have only one finished edge. You can insert the raw edge into a seam or use the trim to finish a garment edge.

Use the following methods to apply these single-edged trims along hemlines, necklines, collars, cuffs or openings:

At an Unfinished Edge:

1. *With right sides together and the finished edge of the trim toward the garment, pin the trim to the garment along the seamline or hemline, so the unfinished edge is on the seam allowance. Stitch the trim in place (A), using a zipper foot attachment to get close to the finished part of the trim.*

2. *If the ends of the trim will not be caught in a seam, allow ½" (13mm) extra at each end to join them. Begin and end your stitching ½" (13mm) from the joining point. Stitch the ends together in a ½" (13mm) seam (B). Trim the seam to ¼" (6mm) and press it open. Finish applying the trim, overlapping the stitches at each end (C).*

3. *Turn the seam allowances to the wrong side of the garment and press. Topstitch the trim in place through all layers. Trim the excess fabric at the seam allowance (D). If your fabric ravels, turn the seam allowances under before you topstitch.*

At a Finished Edge:

1. *With right sides facing up, lap the finished edge of the garment over the unfinished edge of the trim, leaving ½" (13mm) of trim at either end. Pin or baste in place. Edgestitch along the finished edge of the garment, through all thicknesses.*

2. *After the trim is stitched in place, turn each end under ¼" (6mm) to the wrong side, then under ¼" (6mm) again and slip-stitch in place (A).*

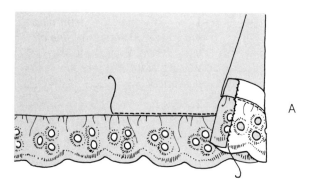

TRIMS ENCLOSED IN A SEAM

Baste the trim in place on one garment section before stitching the seam. Make sure you position the trim face down on one garment section so that the finished portion of the trim is on the garment and any raw edges are on the seam allowance.

The seam allowance width at the unfinished edge varies from trim to trim. Since there is no standard width, position each trim along the seamline so that the entire decorative part of the trim will show after stitching the seam.

1. *Pin the trim in place along the seamline, with the decorative edge toward the body of the garment.*

2. *Hand or machine baste the trim along the seamline (B). If rickrack is used, position and baste it in place so that only half the rickrack will show at the finished edge (C).*

3. *With right sides together, pin the garment sections together*

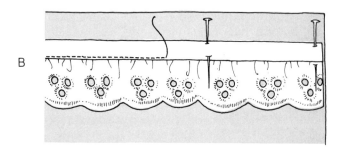

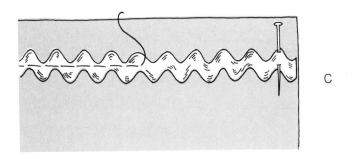

along the seamline. Working with the trimmed garment section on top, machine stitch along the seamline, next to the basting stitches (D).

4. *Press the seam allowances to one side so that the trim faces the correct direction. Grade the fabric seam allowances, if necessary.*

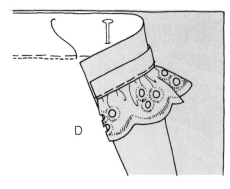

OVERLOCK APPLICATIONS

An overlock machine opens up novel ways to trim children's fashions simultaneously as you finish seams, hems and other edges.

At an Unfinished Edge Use the three-thread overlock stitch for this technique.

1. *With right sides together and the finished edge of the trim toward the body of the garment, pin the trim to the garment along the seamline or hemline.*

2. *Overlock the trim along the seamline. Turn the overlocked edge to the wrong side of the garment and press the trim away from the garment.*

1. *Lightly mark the trim placement line on the right side of your fabric. Fold the fabric wrong sides together along the placement line.*

2. *Position the garment section under the presser foot so that the hem edge is on top and to the left of the cutting knife. Place the straight edge of the lace even with the folded edge of the fabric; then place the ribbon on top of the lace, along the folded edge. Lower the presser foot and stitch so that the right-hand swing of the needle falls over the folded edge. As you stitch, be careful not to catch the ribbon in the stitching or to cut into the fold with the knife.*

For more information:

on Pivoting, see under APPLIQUÉ.

on Basting Tape, Glue Stick, Hand Basting and Machine Basting, see under BASTING.

on Bias Bindings, see under BINDINGS.

on Slipstitching, see under HAND SEWING.

on Edgestitching, Topstitching and Overlock Stitching, see under MACHINE STITCHING.

on Ribbon Trim, see under RIBBONS.

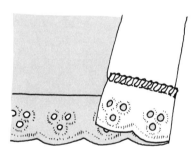

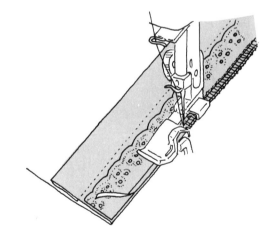

Flat Lace Application This technique requires a flat lace trim with one straight finished edge, narrow ⅛" (3mm)-wide ribbon and some practice. You can vary the decorative effect by using thread that matches or contrasts with the ribbon.

3. *Unfold the fabric and pull the stitches flat.*

Tucks

With tucks, a versatile linear design feature, you can add texture, accent the lines of a garment, control fullness and define shape. In children's clothes, tucks also make a great place to conceal extra length or width to allow for room to grow.

Although a tuck is basically a stitched fabric fold, similar to a pleat, spacing and location variations determine what kind of tuck it is.

▶ **Blind tucks:** *Each tuck touches or overlaps the stitching line of the next one on the outside of the garment.*

▶ **Spaced tucks:** *On the outside of the garment, there is a predetermined space between the folded edge of one tuck and the stitching line of the next one.*

▶ **Pin tucks:** *Each tuck is very narrow, with some space between it and the next one on the outside of the garment.*

▶ **Released** *or* **dart tucks:** *On the inside of the garment, each tuck is stitched to a certain point so that fullness is released at one or both ends of the tuck.*

▶ **Growth tucks:** *These tucks appear on the outside or the inside of the garment and temporarily add extra fabric which will accommodate the child's future growth. As the child grows, you can remove the stitching to release the tuck, adding length or fullness to the garment. For more information on growth tucks, refer to the section on Room to Grow, pages 26–33.*

Blind tucks

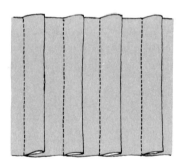

Spaced tucks

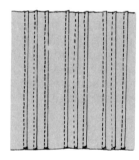

Pin tucks

Released or dart tucks

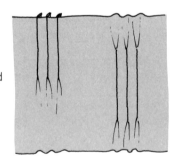

MARKING AND BASTING

To prevent the folds from rippling, make tucks on the straight grain of the fabric. Carefully cut out the garment sections on the straight of grain; mark and stitch the tucks on-grain.

Mark the tucks on whichever side they will be constructed. Use tracing paper and a tracing wheel, tailor's chalk or a marking pen to mark the stitching lines. Whichever method you prefer, test it first on a scrap of your fashion fabric to make sure the markings are removable.

After marking the stitching lines, remove the pattern tissue. Fold the tucks either to the inside or the outside, matching stitching lines, and baste the layers together along the stitching line.

If tracing paper, tailor's chalk or a marking pen are not suitable for your fabric, you can eliminate the need for markings by making a cardboard measurement gauge.

1. *Using your pattern tissue as a guide, determine the width of each tuck and the spacing between the stitching lines of any two tucks. Cut a piece of cardboard as long as the sum of these two measurements. Measuring from one end of the cardboard, mark off the tuck width and make a notch.*

2. *To use the gauge, establish the foldline for the first tuck and place the top of the gauge along this foldline. Using the notch as a guide, make a row of basting stitches parallel to the fold, sliding the gauge along as you stitch.*

3. *For the next tuck, move the gauge so that the bottom is along the stitching line of the first tuck. Fold the fabric along the top of the gauge, then baste it along the notch (A). Repeat this procedure until all the tucks are folded and basted.*

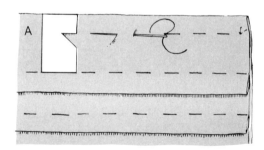

STITCHING

As a general rule, stitch tucks with thread that matches the fabric. To create more visual interest, choose a contrasting-color thread.

1. *To control the finished look of the tuck and the evenness of the stitching, position the garment section so that the upper stitching is the one visible when the tuck is pressed to one side.*

2. *To keep the stitching parallel to the fold, use a stitching guide, such as the marks etched into the throat plate of your machine, a seam guide attachment or a piece of masking tape.*

3. *If you are making released tucks, secure the stitching at the end by backstitching or knotting the thread ends securely (B). If you are pressing the tucks to one side, stitch to the end, pivot the fabric and stitch across the tuck to the fold (C). Backstitch or knot the thread ends to secure.*

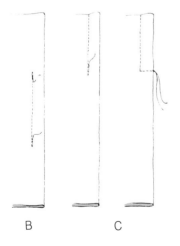

B   C

PRESSING

Press each tuck immediately after you stitch it, or press the entire series of tucks after stitching them. Although it may slow down your sewing, you may get better results if you stitch and press one tuck at a time. Avoid pressing unwanted creases into the surrounding tucks. To prevent puckering, use as little steam as possible.

1. *Press the tuck flat, pressing first on the side of the fabric that will be the underside of the tuck (D).*

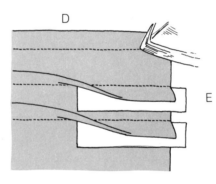

2. *To prevent the tuck fold from creating unwanted indentations in the fabric, put a strip of brown paper between the garment and the tuck; then press the tuck to one side (E).*

3. *If you are making a released tuck, press it along the stitching line only. The released fullness above or below the stitching line should never be pressed flat.*

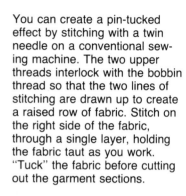

You can create a pin-tucked effect by stitching with a twin needle on a conventional sewing machine. The two upper threads interlock with the bobbin thread so that the two lines of stitching are drawn up to create a raised row of fabric. Stitch on the right side of the fabric, through a single layer, holding the fabric taut as you work. "Tuck" the fabric before cutting out the garment sections.

For more information:

on Basting Techniques, see under BASTING.

on Backstitching, see under MACHINE STITCHING.

see OVERLOCK STITCHING.

on Stitching Guides, see under SEAMS.

on Marking Techniques, see under WHAT TO KNOW BEFORE YOU SEW.

Waistbands

A waistband is meant to hold a skirt or a pair of pants securely in place. Because infants' and toddlers' bodies have no defined waistline, waistbands on their garments usually take the form of elasticized casings, often accompanied by shoulder straps. As children get older, with more shapely bodies, it makes sense to have the traditional applied waistbands on their clothes.

INTERFACING

Interfacing is an essential ingredient in a well-constructed waistband. It prevents the waistband from rolling during wearing and keeps the folded edge crisp and sharp.

For best results, the entire waistband should be interfaced. The fusibles that are specially designed for waistbands, such as Waist Shaper® or Fuse 'n Fold, with perforations or slots along the center foldline, and sometimes along the seamlines, are easy to use. These interfacings

create a crisp edge along the fold of the waistband and help reduce extra bulk at the seams (A).

The waistband interfacing can also be cut from regular fusible interfacing or the sew-in type. Use the waistband pattern piece to cut out the interfacing. If you're using a fusible, trim the interfacing so it extends ⅛" (3mm) into the seam allowances.

To apply fusible interfacing, position it, coated side down, on the wrong side of the waistband and fuse it in place according to the manufacturer's directions.

Pin sew-in interfacing to the wrong side of the waistband, then baste it in place on the seamline all around. Trim the interfacing close to the basting stitches. Using a long running stitch and picking up only one or two garment threads with each stitch, sew the interfacing to the waistband along the foldline.

STRAIGHT WAISTBAND

This waistband is cut on the lengthwise grain of the fabric for the least amount of stretch.

1. *Apply the interfacing to the waistband.*

2. *Turn in the seam allowance on the long unnotched edge, and press it. Trim the seam allowance to ⅜" (10mm) (B).*

3. *With right sides together, pin the waistband to the upper edge of the garment, matching centers and symbols. Adjust ease or gathers, if any, and baste. Stitch, then trim and grade the seam. Press the seam toward the waistband.*

4. *With right sides together, fold the waistband along the foldline. Stitch the ends along the seamline. Trim the seam (C) and clip the corner.*

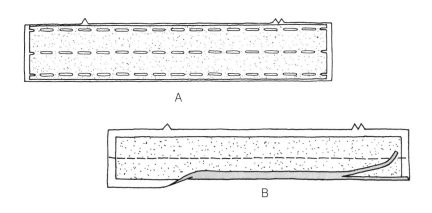

A

B

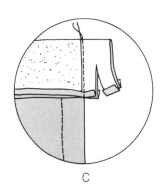

C

185

To use the stitch-in-the-ditch method without using the selvage, cut out the waistband and apply the interfacing. Then trim the seam allowance on the unnotched edge to ⅜" (10mm) and finish it with a machine zigzag or overcast stitch, or an overlock stitch.

5. *Turn the waistband right side out and press it. Slipstitch the pressed edge in place along the seamline and slipstitch the extension edges, if any, together (D).*

6. *If desired, edgestitch and/or topstitch the waistband around all the edges.*

The Stitch-in-the-Ditch Method

One variation of the straight waistband uses the selvage of the fabric to reduce bulk at the waistline seam. The final stitching is concealed in the groove of the waistline seam.

1. *Cut the waistband so that the unnotched edge falls along the selvage and the seam allowance is reduced to ⅜" (10mm) wide (A).*

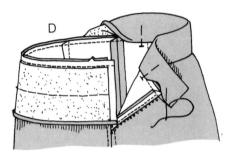

D

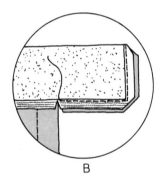

B

the point where the stitching ended. Grade the seam allowances and trim the corners (B).

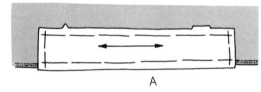

A

2. *Apply the interfacing.*

3. *Construct the waistband according to steps 3 and 4 of the Straight Waistband, page 185.*

4. *With right sides together, fold the waistband along the foldline. Stitch the ends, pivoting at the corner of the underlap and ending at the finished edge of the garment. Make a diagonal clip in the underlap seam allowances just to, but not through,*

5. *Turn the waistband to the inside and press. Pin the waistband in place, matching seamlines and making sure the selvage edge extends ⅜" (10mm) below the seamline. Tuck in the cut ends of the selvage; then, with the right side of the garment facing up, stitch in the groove of the seamline, securing the selvage of the waistband as you stitch (C).*

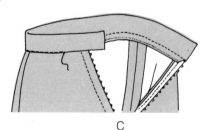

C

For more information:

on Glue Stick and Hand Basting, see under BASTING.

on Running Stitch and Slipstitch, see under HAND SEWING.

on Fusible and Sew-in Interfacing, see under INTERFACING.

on Grading and Trimming, see under SEAMS.

Zippers

There are many good reasons to put zippers in children's garments. They are a strong, secure fastener that always stays neat and in place. There are no small pieces to come loose and find their way into tiny mouths. And, they are an easy-to-use fastener for those who are just learning to dress themselves. If the pull-tab is too small for little fingers to maneuver, add a bit of ribbon, a tassel or decorative zipper pull.

CENTERED ZIPPERS

When the child's garment has a zipper, it is usually a centered zipper. For easy installation, insert the zipper before attaching any intersecting garment sections, such as facings, collars or waistbands.

1. *Stitch the seam, leaving an opening above the symbol. Machine baste along the seamline above the symbol, then press the seam open (A).*

2. *Open the zipper, place it face down on the extended seam allowance of the zipper opening with the zipper teeth on the seamline and pin in place. Machine baste down the center of the zipper tape, keeping the garment free (B).*

3. *Close the zipper and turn the pull-tab up. Spread the garment flat, with the wrong side facing you. Hand baste a scant ¼" (6mm) from the teeth on both sides of the zipper and across the lower edge (C). For accuracy, measure as you baste.*

4. *On the right side of the garment, and using a zipper foot, stitch just next to the basting, through all thicknesses (D). To keep the fabric from puckering, stitch both sides of the zipper in the same direction. Remove the basting.*

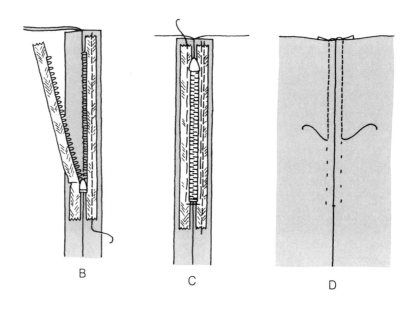

A

B

C

D

187

MOCK FLY FRONT

The *mock* fly front zipper method looks like a *tailored* fly front zipper, but has the advantage of fewer steps. If this application is a design feature on your pattern, the pattern tissue has markings for the underlap and overlap extensions.

Before you begin, mark the topstitching line on the right side of the garment with disappearing dressmaker's carbon and a tracing wheel, a water soluble marking pen, tailor's chalk or a line of hand basting stitches. *Note:* These directions and illustrations are for a girl's garment. For a boy's and teen boy's garment, the zipper would be reversed.

1. *Stitch the center front seam from the symbol that indicates the end of the zipper to the symbol that marks the approximate middle of the center front crotch curve. Machine baste along the seamline from the zipper symbol to the upper edge of the garment section (A).*

2. *Turn the left front extension to the wrong side along the fold-line and press. Place the closed zipper face up under the left front extension, matching the zipper stop with the indicated marking and keeping the zipper teeth close to the pressed edge. Hand baste the zipper in place, then machine stitch it (B).*

3. *Fold the zipper and left front extension over so that they are face down on the right front extension. Keeping the garment front free, stitch the remaining zipper tape to the right front extension only (C).*

4. *Turn the right front extension toward the garment front and hand baste in place along the marked stitching line (D).*

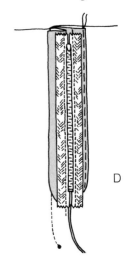

5. *On the right side of the garment, secure the right front extension by topstitching along the marked stitching line. Stitch through all the layers, including the seam allowance and zipper tape near the bottom of the curve (E).*

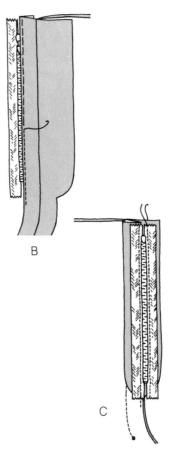

B

C

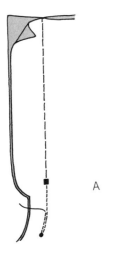

A

E

SEPARATING ZIPPER

A separating zipper—one that comes apart at the bottom—is a favorite closure for sporty jackets and coats. Because the zipper separates, the garment is easier to put on and take off—a plus when dressing wiggly children!

1. *Baste the front opening edges together along the seamline. Press the seam allowances open (A).*

2. *Center the closed zipper face down over the front opening edges, placing the zipper stop at* the symbol. Hand baste the zipper in place the desired distance from the zipper teeth on both sides of the zipper (B). For accuracy, measure as you baste.

3. *If the garment is unlined, turn it to the right side and, using a zipper foot, stitch just next to the basting (C). For a lined garment, prepare and attach the lining according to the pattern instructions, then stitch the zipper in place on the outside of the garment. Remove all basting stitches.*

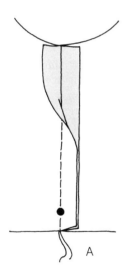

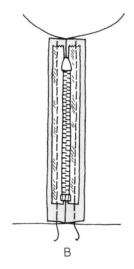

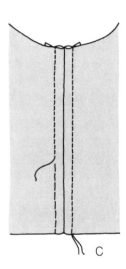

For easy removal later, clip the basting stitches at the bottom of the zipper opening and every 2" (5cm). Use pointed tweezers to remove the stitches once the zipper is installed.

SHORTENING A ZIPPER

Your pattern instructions tell you
the correct length of zipper to
use for the garment you're making. However, if you can't find
the right color zipper in the right
length, purchase a longer zipper and shorten it.

You can shorten most types
of zippers from the bottom, but
you must shorten a *separating*
zipper from the top.

To shorten from the bottom:

▶ *Place the closed zipper along
the opening edge with the pull-
tab below the seamline.*

▶ *Mark the position of the new
zipper stop. Whipstitch across
the teeth at this marking.*

▶ *Cut off the excess zipper ¾"
(20mm) below the new stop (A).*

To shorten from the top:

▶ *Place the closed zipper along
the opening edge with the stop at
the marking that indicates the
end of the zipper opening.*

▶ *Open the zipper a little bit
until the pull-tab is below the
seamline.*

▶ *Whipstitch over the teeth on
each side of the zipper just above
the pull-tab.*

▶ *Cut off the excess zipper ¾"
(20mm) above the whipstitches
(B).*

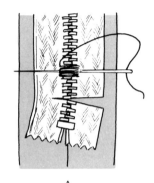

A

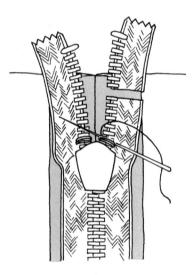

B

For more information:

see BASTING.

on Whipstitch, see under HAND
SEWING.

on Edgestitching and Topstitching, see under MACHINE STITCH-
ING.

on Marking Techniques, see under WHAT TO KNOW BEFORE YOU
SEW.

Index